Dear Principal Shelby,   9/9/22
   It has been an honor to
serve under your leadership.
You serve as a source of inspirati
and hope for your students +
staff. Let's stay connected
Personally and professionally.
   I would love to be able to
support your students in some
Copacity. Wishing you all the best,
                          Rochelle

SIMPLY
COMPLEX

Unmask
the
Persona
and
Show
the
World
**the Best
of You!**

SIMPLY COMPLEX

LEADING OUT OF AUTHENTICITY

ROCHELLE ARMSTRONG

ISBN print 978-1-7364682-0-3

ISBN epub 978-1-7364682-1-0

Contents

Introduction _____ 7

Pillar I: Environment _____ 15

Pillar II: DNA _____ 33

Pillar III: Identity _____ 43

Pillar IV: Personality_____ 55

Pillar V: Love _____ 75

Pillar VI: Stand up! _____ 87

Pillar VII: Names_____ 95

Pillar VIII: Self-Love _____ 105

Pillar IX: Self-Acceptance_____ 113

Pillar X: Self-Worth _____ 129

Pillar XI: Authenticity_____ 137

Pillar XII: Simply Complex _____ 159

Acknowledgments _____ 167

Endnotes _____ 169

Introduction

To know thyself is the beginning of wisdom.
—Socrates

What was your greatest fear growing up? Spiders? Snakes? Clowns? Being in the dark?

Well, next to imagining that my grandma would die one day, I think my greatest fear was being mediocre, average, or simple. A strange fear? Yes, there really are people in the world who fear being average—at least one person: me. Given my nature, interestingly enough, it doesn't make sense to me. If I'm being honest with you (and true to myself), I'm an introvert who learned to operate as an extrovert. One might call me an ambivert—someone who is a blend of both. Basically, I'm sociable, but I need time to recharge alone. At any rate, I prefer not to be in the spotlight or the center of attention.

One of my oldest memories is when I was in the chorus at Meyzeek Middle School. We had a performance at a shopping center called The Galleria in downtown Louisville, Kentucky. Days before the concert, I was so nervous, I lost my appetite. My stomach was in knots. You would have thought that I was going to be the headliner, because I rehearsed my lines over and over again about the excuse (or lie) I was going to tell to get out of going to the performance.

First, I thought, I could act sick. A commonly used excuse, but not highly imaginative. Then I thought, "How convenient would it be if we could get a snow day?" That way, I wouldn't have to tell a lie. Better yet, maybe the concert would get canceled, due to whatever, just canceled. I imagine this sort of thing happens all the time. Ever been there? You had this big meeting, game, test, or special occasion coming up, and all you could think about was how you could get out of it?

All these thoughts roamed through my mind as I anxiously awaited the upcoming two-week Christmas break that I couldn't get to without first singing in the program. Now, fast forward to the morning of the concert. I was ready to call in my well-rehearsed sick day, since I couldn't magically make twelve inches of snow appear and canceling the performance was out of the question. Nervously, I didn't want to say that I was sick because acting comes with the dramatization of appearing sick, and performing is not a gift of mine.

So, before the lines could flow from my lips like a well-rehearsed actress, the so-called "lie" of being sick was suppressed by guilt and shame. I froze up. I couldn't do it. The show must go on—with me. Thankfully, I was *not* the headliner at the concert, but I still had to show up! Nervous energy and all. I hid back as far as I could in the alto section, lip-synching to all the lyrics.

What a sigh of relief when it was over. I wish I could say that I enjoyed it once I got over my fear, but I didn't. As a matter of fact, I never got over my fear. I simply performed, being scared stiff.

I am not suggesting that being in the spotlight or being the center of attention is synonymous with greatness, but how would anyone know about the great impact you've made or are making if no one knows who you are?

Another example of my internal contradiction of fearing being mediocre yet being too shy and insecure to be in the spotlight was around the age of ten. We had a youth pageant at church. Let's be clear: this was no beauty pageant. Actually, the criteria for winning was primarily based on patrons and sponsorships because it was a fundraiser to raise money for the youth. Where are people most likely to be approached to support a fundraiser? Did you say work? Correct. Sure, you'll ask family, neighbors, church, or groups you belong to, but your number one target is people who have money, right?

Given that my grandma didn't work, we had a small family in Louisville, and the other youth would potentially be asking for donations from other members of the church, surely my chances of winning were slim. In addition to sponsorships, other criteria had to be met to even participate in the pageant. It was pivotal for youth leaders to show the benefits of having youth in the program. Nominees were known by adults and peers for having good character, showing manners, helping others, using good judgment, and making good grades in school. Just like an election, members of the church were given detailed descriptions of each nominee and could donate publicly or anonymously.

Unbeknownst to me, my grandma was quite influential and persuasive because I didn't ask anyone for a donation. I'll never forget the day that the votes came in. To my dismay, I won.

Yes, I said, "To my dismay." Can you imagine what winning meant for this shy, timid, insecure girl? That's right, I had to walk down the red carpet from the rear of the church to right in front of the altar, where I would be crowned with a tiara and announced as the winner. Talk about one of the most awkward moments of my life! Maybe I watched too much television, because I thought there was a certain rhythm or pacing when walking to be crowned. If there was, I never figured it out. I did some sort of awkward "take two steps, pause, two steps, pause" all the way down the aisle until I made it to the altar. Minus the blindfold, I felt like I was walking the plank. There was nothing about my posture or appearance that would be mistaken for royalty or greatness.

Truthfully, I didn't want to win for the same reason I didn't want to sing in the Christmas performance. I didn't want to be the center of attention. Until this day, when asked, "How do you like to be recognized?" my response is, "In private," or maybe in a small group, depending on the dynamics. Don't be mistaken. I love expressions of appreciation, even special attention, just not a parade. Yet here I was: on public display for all to see. At least at the Christmas performance, I could hide, but not at the pageant. Life is funny that way. Have you ever been nervous about getting a yes to a wonderful opportunity? You're convinced you don't want it (perhaps out of fear), but in your gut, you know it's going to happen. That's what happened to me.

My life has always been simply complex in an "It shouldn't be me. Why would it be me? But yes, it is me" type of way. There's a part of me that wants to be simple because simple goes under the radar. Simple is safe. Simple is likable. Simple is accepted. And, as much as I would like to keep my life simple, even at the risk of being mediocre, I've never been able to ignore or outrun the silent whisper in my soul saying "Greater." What about you?

Simply Complex is about self-discovery. I believe that *everyone* has a purpose, but often we have dreams deferred or don't dream at all. Many of us have become paralyzed by a negative self-image as a result of dysfunctional families, unhealthy/abusive relationships, mistakes, or poor decisions. Then, unconsciously or knowingly, we go through society introducing people to our persona at work, school, church, or social gatherings. Seems harmless enough, right?

Perhaps there's no harm done in everyday superficial interactions, but could your inauthenticity lessen your effectiveness as a leader? Would you not agree that it's imperative to build trust with the people you lead at your home or as part of a sports team, classroom, or boardroom?

To build trust, you have to remove your mask, drop the persona, and lead from a place of *authenticity*. Does the thought of unmasking—revealing your flawed, imperfect identity—seem scary? Can you imagine yourself being that vulnerable? Vulnerability takes courage, doesn't it? According to the well-known author and speaker Brené Brown, "Courage and fear are not mutually exclusive. Most of us feel brave and afraid at the same time."[1]

Can you relate? If so, you're not alone. Imagine me holding your hand as we go on this journey together. It doesn't get more vulnerable than writing a book about how you've masked to be accepted and fit in. You can only imagine the vulnerability and courage it took for me to share my journey of inauthenticity with you. The reason I did is because I believe that you too want to be free to display and embrace the person you were created to be. Isn't it less scary if we unmask together?

Before we go on this journey together, we must build a strong foundation. If not, just like any other form of written or verbal inspiration, shortly after the book ends or the conference is over, we'll gradually retreat to the same counterproductive attitude and behaviors. Now that we've agreed that we're going to unmask and lead out of authenticity, we need to put some pillars in place so when life throws us curve balls and whirlwinds, we'll have a shield of protection in place.

The purpose of pillars in a relationship or a house is to provide reliable, essential support. But have you ever been in a building, possibly a basement with poles or pillars, and they were more of a distraction? The company I used to work for had a training room that was dedicated to leadership and team development because it was easy to arrange the room with or without tables. There were no computers installed, which made it great for team-building activities and discussions that occasionally required people to get up and move around. However, there was a huge pillar at the front of the room that made it difficult to set up the room so that everyone could see the facilitator and their presentation on the overhead.

What I didn't share is that we could've put in a request for new equipment, chairs, tables, or anything else that would help create an environment conducive to an optimal learning experience. But why do you think nobody ever put in a request to remove that pillar? That's right—the pillar was needed to keep the rest of the structure in place.

Often, just like that pillar keeping the structure in place, those things in life that may seem like distractions or barriers are essential to our foundation and character-building, which will contribute to our overall success. For example, going to therapy to get help for childhood trauma could appear to be a distraction if you're trying to build a new business or relationship. But, left unchecked, repressed experiences can rise up and leak out of us in unhealthy ways, unintentionally hindering our goals. In this book, the Twelve Pillars serve as the foundation needed for discovering your self, embracing your authentic self, and leading out of authenticity.

Pillar I: Environment

If you're going through hell, keep going.
—Winston Churchill

The first pillar, your environment, plays a significant role in shaping your identity. When you graced the world with your presence as someone's beautiful bundle of joy, do you remember putting in a request about where you wanted to live? No. Neither do I. That decision was already made by the person or persons who would be raising you. Their decision was probably based on personal preference and/or social economics. But environment isn't limited to one's home or neighborhood. Here are several aspects that may contribute to an environment:

- **People** (personality, age, sense of style, ethnicity, traditions, race, or gender)

- **Stores** (grocery stores, retail stores, convenience stores, drug stores, liquor stores, comic bookstores, gas stations, farmers markets)

- **Structures** (condos, houses, apartments, patio homes)

- **Surroundings** (lawns, trees, privacy fences, bars on windows, sidewalks, dirt roads)

- **Organisms** (domestic animals, farm animals, gardens, flowers)

Everything in that environment influences who you are today, how you make decisions, and how you judge yourself and others. It can become the standard of how you see the world. Good or bad, you didn't choose your environment. It doesn't define you, but trying to disassociate from it can cost you some of your authenticity. Therefore, choose to draw strength from your environment.

What makes you, *you*? Who did you get your harmonious, controlling, witty, or charming personality from? Are you quick to speak and slow to listen? Do you like to communicate and keep the peace? Does everything have to have its proper place and order in your life? Do you like debating for the sake of being right? Surely you can relate to one, maybe two, of these.

Even so, isn't there still more to you? Your personality is only part of your identity. From the time you entered into your mother's womb, the person you are today was being formed, starting with your DNA. As the nature-versus-nurture debate continues, for the sake of argument, let's entertain the theory that nature (genetics) and nurture (environment) play a role in shaping your behavior and personality.

Did you know that 2.7 million children in the United States have an incarcerated parent? That is one in twenty-eight children, according to Rutgers University's National Resource Center on Children and Families of the Incarcerated. Approximately 12 percent of children in the United States live with at least one parent who is dependent on or addicted to alcohol or drugs. And, according to the

National Survey of Children's Exposure to Violence, one in four children (26 percent) are exposed to some form of family violence during their lifetime.[2] By the age of eleven, I had experienced all three. According to that data, because of my DNA and environment, that would have made me a statistic or an at-risk youth.[3]

I was told that when I was two years of age, my older sister (who is two years older than me) and I were brought to Louisville by my mother to visit our paternal grandmother for the summer. She never came back for us. Given that we've lived in Louisville most of our lives, there has to be some truth to that story, but maybe it doesn't tell the entire story. (Later in life, my mom got to share her version of the story, which I'll also share with you, if you choose to stay tuned.) The stories will be true to the best of my recollection, as they are still deeply felt today. With the thought of unmasking so many untold truths, it feels like ripping off Band-Aids from partially healed wounds. But if I'm going to encourage you to unmask and lead out of authenticity, it has to start with me.

To help you better understand what makes leading out of authenticity so simply complex, I'm going to share with you all my names that I'll refer to as personas. Before introducing you to Rochelle (my middle name and current public persona), I have to introduce you to Lady (one of my nicknames and the persona that has had the greatest impact on my life).

Nicknames are common for a lot of people; some have absolutely no meaning (like the one we gave our youngest daughter, Dejah, when she was a baby, which is Booty). Yet other nicknames may be given because you remind the "namer" of something or someone. Do you have a nickname(s) or did you give a nickname to a child? If so, why?

In my case, I was told that my mother gave me the nickname Lady because when I was a little girl, I acted like a lady. One example my mom shared with me is that when I was barely two years old, I threw a fit because mustard got on my clothes. She said I wanted to always be neat and clean. This hasn't changed much for me as an adult. Needless to say, it wasn't only cleanliness that made my mom call me Lady. Many toddlers could've been given that nickname. In addition to my wanting to be spot-free, she said that my proper diction and mannerisms reminded her of a little lady. Not taking any votes or opinions from others, the decision was made: My mom deemed Lady a suitable nickname for me.

Do you have an alter ego or a persona that you can relate to? A persona can be a different side of you that may even surprise you but gives you the courage to show up in the world without fear of rejection. Beyoncé refers to her alter ego as Sasha Fierce. Sasha Fierce is the singer, dancer, entertainer, and actor whom Beyoncé channels to perform on the celebrity platform that leaves fans around the world mesmerized. I'm inspired by her work ethic, but Sasha Fierce is not a persona that fully resonates with me. Kendrick Lamar—aka Kungfu Kenny—on the other hand, uses lyrics in his song "DNA" that I can relate to.

I have an appreciation for hip hop and even some rap that my former and evolved circle of friends does not. Songs like "DNA" tell tales of a life that I can identify with. It tells a story of being born into a world of hardship and pain yet having the fortitude to live through it. What makes music so universal is beyond the beats that you bop your head or tap your foot to. It surpasses how the rhythm of each musical chord makes you feel. If you silence your mind and body long enough and listen to the lyrics, you'll hear a story, no matter the genre of music, that reminds you that you're not alone. Do you have a song or genre of music that you can relate to?

Lady and my sister, Neki, grew up in a small one-bedroom shotgun house in a part of town called Smoketown. If you're not familiar with Louisville, envision just about any inner-city neighborhood, or what some might call the ghetto or hood. Smoketown is a neighborhood one mile southeast of downtown Louisville. It has been a historically black neighborhood since the Civil War. According to an 1871 directory, Smoketown got its name from being located in Louisville's brickyards. This was thanks to a giant deposit of clay in the ground. The kilns used in brickyards produced smoke as well as bricks.[4] Since we're talking about identity and authenticity, I thought I'd share a fun fact about where Smoketown got its identity from.

Now, back to Lady's identity. When my grandfather bought the cozy little house, perfect for two, I'm sure he had no idea that two of his step-grandchildren would eventually be calling this place home. As such, there only was one bedroom, which was rightfully for Grandma and Grandpa, which meant that Neki and Lady would become roomies, sleeping on the living room floor with a pile of blankets. For people who are privileged enough to have their own bedroom, or at least their own bed, this could sound like less-than-desirable living conditions. However, when you grow up poor, you become adaptable and learn to get creative with your situation. To that end, Neki and Lady looked forward to bedtime so that they could make tents out of blankets and/or share scary stories under the covers.

Another reason I personally looked forward to bedtime was so I could use my vivid imagination. Before I would doze off, I would fantasize about how I wanted my life to be. This would become my reality, if only in a dream. I was no older than nine or ten years old, but I imagined that I was married to Malcolm-Jamal Warner from *The Cosby Show* (I'm smiling as I'm typing this). We lived in an enormous house with two beautiful kids. Malcolm was still an actor and I was an attorney, like Perry Mason. A little-known fact for millennial readers: Perry Mason was a high-profile attorney who was the white male version of Annalise Keating on the prime-time show *How to Get Away with Murder*.

One of the best Christmases from Lady's childhood was when I walked to the Salvation Army with my grandmother, and we were given two gigantic black garbage bags full of toys. Lady's grandmother was no fancy lady who believed in bells and whistles, so the notion of actually removing the toys from the garbage bags and wrapping them was not an option. Moreover, it didn't take away from it being one of the most memorable Christmases I had as a child. Board games like Chutes and Ladders, Operation, and Candy Land put a gigantic smile on Lady's and Neki's faces. It didn't matter that other kids came to school bragging about getting the latest gaming system called Atari, because if we wanted to play games like Donkey Kong and Pac Man, we'd just go over to our younger cousin Jawana's house.

During this time, life for Lady was good, until I found out that Neki would be leaving to temporarily stay with Uncle James and Aunt Temp. And although I would miss my sister dearly, Lady still favored staying with Grandma. I loved my grandmother more than life itself and couldn't imagine life without her.

One night, my grandmother was admitted to St. Anthony's Hospital for some illness that I can't recall. Not knowing the seriousness of her condition or when she would come home, Lady stood in the front yard of the minuscule shotgun house (that was literally called The Little House), gazing up at the dark blue sky, trying to see God through what seemed like a billion stars. Setting diplomacy and filters aside, I told God boldly and directly, "Please bring my grandma home, and never take her away again." God answered part of that request, because shortly after that night, Grandma came home from the hospital. But when she came home, she didn't bestow big hugs or terms of endearment. Margaret wasn't the most affectionate woman. But I knew that I was deeply loved and Grandma's favorite.

As I recall this part of Lady's story, it should be crystal clear, black and white, but it's sort of blurry and gray. It was a sunny afternoon that could have been a beautiful summer day, but not remembering the exact date, it could have been a beautiful fall day. What is clear is that the weather was nice and the sun was shining brightly, at least outdoors. What was not so pleasant about this day was that my grandmother had decided to divorce my grandfather and move back into her house (The Big House) across the alley from his house.

Interestingly enough, we had been staying at my grandma's house, but as a kid, I didn't really know why. Back then, adults were not open with kids about personal issues, so I had no idea they were getting a divorce. All I knew was that just about every weekend, Grandma and Grandpa would have friends over to play cards, listen to loud old-school music, and drink spirits. My grandfather was known to drink what I heard Grandma refer to as "the hard liquor" that would more times than not turn him into a mean drunk.

For a lack of better words, he would act like a fool! Grandma and Grandpa were registered to carry a concealed weapon; they both had guns. When Grandpa got drunk, he would place his gun on his end of the coffee table. But, being the fearless, no-nonsense woman Grandma was, she would emulate him, reminding him that she had a gun too.

I have no memory of any physical abuse, but when Grandpa got drunk, verbal fireworks sparked in the room as if it were the fourth of July. Every Friday night (Grandpa's payday), he'd unintentionally kick off a spectacular, undesired firework show. Woefully, these colorful sparks were not as pretty and exciting as the ones we see on the day we Americans celebrate independence.

For Lady, Neki, and Grandma, this show was not due

to end—until they went to church on Sunday morning. This became our norm. Lady and Neki never thought to share the arguments or their seeing the firearms with their aunts and uncles because they didn't witness any physical violence. Not to mention, their grandparents made it clear that "What goes on in this house, stays in this house!" But none of this changed how Lady grew to dread the day of the week (Friday) that most working people looked forward to. Instead, Lady and Neki fearfully awaited the storm Grandpa would bring once the drinking started.

Today, a therapist would label that environment as dysfunctional, but Lady didn't have that word in her vocabulary back then. Later, Neki and Lady found out that this was not normal at all. Their aunts and uncles lovingly yet disappointedly expressed how they should've told one of them about the gun intimidation and arguments every weekend. Over the years, I often wondered if I could've spared everyone, especially myself, an irreplaceable void and inconsolable pain by sharing the dysfunctional behaviors and interactions, despite being told not to. "If only I wasn't such a sheepish little girl."

Going back to that beautiful sunny day, Lady (who was also called Cookie by her grandmother) answered the phone and heard her grandma calmly say, "Cookie, come over here and help me get my things out of his house." One thing Lady knew about her grandmother was that if she asked you to do something, you better do it immediately, no questions asked! Grandma wasn't going to say it twice. Lady hurried over to Grandpa's house.

She skipped swiftly yet cheerfully through Grandma's backyard, quickly approaching Grandpa's house. But before Lady reached his front door, only a few feet away, she heard a gunshot.

Without hesitation, this turned Lady's skip into a run. Lady ran as fast as she could toward Grandpa's house. Regrettably, not fast enough. Lady heard another gunshot before making it to the front door. Finally, she made it! But when she opened the front door, it was too late: Grandma sat in front of the door, her head tilted and blood running down her face.

It was obvious that he had shot her before she could make it out the door. It was like Grandma and Lady were running toward each other, but their paths would never cross again. The separation ended immediately when Lady opened the glass screen door and Grandma didn't walk through it.

What if she had arrived mere seconds sooner? What if? Survivor's guilt immediately kicked in. Lady immediately thought, "Why didn't he shoot me too?" It was too late. No time for self-pity. No time to overthink.

"But wait a minute," she thought. "Where is he?" He had to still be in the house, but she didn't see him. Everything happened so fast, including Lady running back to The Big House for help. Before going in, Lady slammed her hands against the screen door. Glass shattered everywhere. Still, no time to panic. No time for pain. Without further delay, Lady called 911, got Neki (the only person at home), and ran back to The Little House.

What a resounding cry! Lady's scream was so loud and chilling, people started running to the house from everywhere. When the police arrived, the cry was so piercing that they asked a neighbor to calm her down or they'd have to remove her from the premises because it was distracting them from their investigation. Unfortunately, when Grandma's children and the ambulance got there, nothing could be done to revive her.

I will never forget riding in the yellow Monte Carlo with dark-tinted windows with my uncle Charles and my sister, when my uncle looked in the rear-view mirror with tears rolling down his face and said, "Momma's brain-dead."

A few days later, Grandma was taken off the ventilator and pronounced dead. Lady and Neki were orphans again, faced with needing new guardianship and a place to stay. This forced their courageous young single uncle Charles to step up to the plate and finish raising his nieces. He did the best he could, but with limited resources and inexperience with raising teenage girls, things would be nothing short of challenging from this point on.

A few years after Grandma's death, Lady's identity was being brutally shaped without permission or regard. Being the only witness, I had to testify at Grandpa's trial.

If finding her grandmother shot to death, testifying at her grandfather's trial, and instantly adjusting to new guardianship wasn't enough to start shaping what would be a cold, guarded, rebellious, and angry identity, becoming pregnant by a man five years Lady's senior certainly would.

One day, I was outside playing with a friend in front

of the apartment where we lived, wearing a yellow t-shirt, denim shorts, and tennis shoes. Unsuspiciously, a guy from the neighborhood walked by while bouncing a basketball, said "What's up?" and disappeared. We didn't give him a second thought. We continued to talk and play, and shortly after, went into the apartment, ate dinner, and went to bed.

To my devastating surprise, the same guy who had walked past earlier was now on top of me, telling me to be quiet as he forced himself on me. From that day forward, he would continue to climb through the window in the middle of the night and have sex with me, a blank look on his face, barely saying a word.

Are you wondering why I didn't say anything? Like most people in that situation (or should we say a child, in Lady's case), there's guilt, shame, embarrassment, unworthiness, and the thought "Am I going to get in trouble?" I was also incredibly shy and easily embarrassed; I hid everything, even when I started my menstrual cycle. Since I did not have a relationship with an adult who I felt comfortable with, when I started my menstrual cycle, I had to get creative with protection (ladies, you know what we use for protection when Mother Nature comes by surprise) until my grandmother saw the evidence of a period when she was washing clothes. For someone who can't keep my mouth shut today, if you didn't ask or see it for yourself, Lady wasn't telling *anybody* anything!

To my grandfather's surprise, at the trial, I was visibly pregnant. I'll never forget the pain and guilt in his eyes. If his eyes could speak, they would have said, "What have I done? I'm so sorry!" One of Grandpa's favorite sayings was "I run a tight ship around here," and he did. In other words, Lady and Neki lived in a very strict, highly respected, and well-disciplined home. Therefore, there was no doubt in Grandpa's mind that if he hadn't done the unthinkable, unforgettable—and to some, unforgivable—act of rage, Lady would *not* be pregnant.

Since his eyes couldn't speak and he couldn't talk to her at the trial, he had his sister give Lady some money to buy necessities for her unborn child. Other than being nervous and not well-spoken on the stand in court, I can't remember much about that day. All I know is that he went to prison for the rest of his life, and Lady would never see or hear from him again. Now Grandma was gone, Grandpa too, and her mother and father were nowhere to be found.

I was like a sheep without a shepherd. This man was able to get in and out of that apartment for months without being detected. Even worse, because I had become quite the magician at keeping myself invisible, nobody noticed that I was pregnant. I hid the pregnancy for eight months! That meant no prenatal visits, no vitamins, not even an ultrasound. There were a few times that Uncle Wilbur mentioned that something about me looked different, but pregnancy never came up. But when Uncle Charles took me to the clinic to consider options, the baby was full term, so no abortion and no adoption!

His existence in the world was meant to be. That baby, who is now a healthy, strong, intelligent man, gave Lady a reason to live.

Moment of Personal Reflection

Whew! Let's exhale. Talk about vulnerability. Not sure how all that was able to come out of me. I guess you could say that I just took the first step in modeling this idea of leading out of authenticity.

Now that I've opened up and let you in, I'm expecting *you* to open up and be vulnerable too. The difference for you is that until you're ready - if you are ever ready - you only have to open up and be honest with yourself. If you read the introduction, I asked you to take my hand so that we could go on this journey together. Imagine me still holding your hand.

Do you like journaling? If journaling sounds too formal, you can write your responses on a sheet of paper, index card, napkin, or your hand. However, if you enjoy journaling, like me, bookmark or dog-ear this page and go get your journal.

It can be scary revisiting the environment we grew up in, so if bringing up your past is too uncomfortable or painful, feel free to skip over the activities in the Moment of Reflections and move to the next chapter. But for those of you who are emotionally able to reflect and see how your past could be defining your present and preventing you from leading out of authenticity, take a moment to answer or ponder on the next few questions.

1. What type of environment did you grow up in? How has that environment shaped your identity?

    _____

    _____

2. What are some of the things you took from your environment that you would never change? Why?

    _____

    _____

3. What are some things from your environment that you had to change? Why?

    _____

    _____

4. What is the most valuable lesson you learned from your environment?

    _____

    _____

Need more space? Turn to page 32.

Removing Your Mask

Before you can embrace your true identity and lead out of authenticity, you have to remove your mask. To remove your mask, you have to be honest with yourself about your past and where you come from. A lot of people are crippled by their past, and it prevents them from walking in their purpose and being successful.

I'll never forget one of the coaching sessions I was facilitating for mid-level managers. One of the leaders, Scott, said he was struggling with work-life balance because when he was growing up, his dad was always at work. He went on to say that his father provided a huge, beautiful home for them, he and his siblings got the best education that money could buy, and they stayed nicely dressed in the latest sneakers and clothes. But they desperately longed for their father's time and affection. As a result, now that Scott's a leader, he struggles with working anything over forty hours, although his role often requires him to do so.

Why do you think that is? You're right: Scott's afraid that his children will feel neglected by him the same way he felt neglected by his father. Based on the type of environment he grew up in, he was starting to question if he wanted to stay in his leadership role, because he cared more about what his children thought of him than about the position. However, once I started probing deeper, I discovered that he was the breadwinner of his family and his wife was a stay-at-home mom. He took pride in being the provider and his wife being able to live her dream of staying home with their children.

It was clear to me that stepping down from his position wasn't an option, especially given that Scott enjoyed leading people. But guess what? Those words never came out of my mouth. I didn't have to tell him that he didn't need to step down. After he opened up, shared his story, and acknowledged his fear, he told me that he didn't want to step down, but he wanted to figure out a way to have a better work-life balance.

From there, I was able to customize his coaching sessions, using some of Stephen Covey's time management suggestions. The only reason most leaders in his department had to work overtime was because they weren't able to do one-on-ones with their employees, learn the newly implemented system, and help the team meet their goals within an eight-hour day (your life story, right?). With that in mind, in addition to focusing on time management, I sent him a time-tracker so that he could identify how he was spending his time. This allowed him to account for some time-wasters, such as answering the same questions over and over from the same agents instead of instructing them to read the guidelines they should have been following for that particular process.

Before our coaching sessions, Scott wanted to step down from his leadership role—not because he didn't enjoy it, not because he wasn't good at it, but because he was crippled by an experience from the environment he grew up in. The fear of ending up like his father had shaped his identity and how he viewed himself. By acknowledging the truth that his father was a workaholic, but not allowing that experience to define him, he has since been promoted to a director position. From what I've been told, he still manages his time well enough to work an eight- or nine-hour workday (with a few exceptions during peak seasons), have date nights with his wife, and make it to his son's lacrosse games. More importantly, he has been leading out of authenticity, which he says has made him "more approachable and invested in the people he leads."

A lot of people have baggage from the environment they grew up in, but try not to let past experiences define you. What you don't manage will manage you.

Reflections

Pillar II: DNA

It's not how you start that's
important, but how you finish.
—Jim George

It doesn't take science to prove that our second pillar, DNA, has just as much influence on our identity and how we see the world as the environment does. Like most theories, there will always be debate about whether behavior and personality are caused primarily by nature or nurture. Therefore, think about who you are and how you see the world. Any connection to your DNA? Have you ever met someone whose biological parents never raised them, but when they met them later in life, they had their mannerisms and sense of humor and similar interests? Maybe that person is you.

The point I'm making is that no matter how smart, gifted, or talented you are, your DNA contributes to how you see yourself. Pillar II is to affirm to you: there's more to you than your DNA, which is why it can't define you.

In the spirit of authenticity, here's full transparency: I wanted to open this chapter with a few verses from Kendrick Lamar's song "DNA" because, being the prolific lyricist he is, the lyrics in his song describe the story of my DNA in a much more eloquent way than I believe I can, but given that copyright could be an issue, I'll have to enlighten you on my DNA in a less provocative way.

If you're anything like me, people see the person that you are today but can't imagine what you've been through or where you come from. What shaped you? What formed you? As a forty-six-year-old middle-class woman who worked in corporate America for nearly three decades with a master's degree in business communication and married to a pastor, people who have never been introduced to Lady feel comfortable, even safe around me. But then there are those three little letters: DNA; who I come from.

The modern-day Bonnie and Clyde: Alvin and Debbie, my parents. I don't know nor can I say what types of criminal activities they may have been involved in, but they both lived complicated lives. Their impulsive and careless behavior would eventually lead to drugs and run-ins with the law. They never married. Even to this day, I don't know how long they were a couple. All I know is that they had two children together and more children with other people, but other than my sister Neki (same mother and father) and my brother Maund (same mother, different father), I don't have a relationship with any of them. There's a part of me that would like to find them and reach out to them, but the other part is fearful of the burden it could carry. For now, my soul finds rest by leaving well enough alone.

My mother is deceased. May her soul rest in peace. She died several years ago at the age of fifty-four. When she died, so did my hope of having a healthy mother-daughter relationship. This does not imply that we didn't have a relationship. On the contrary, we had almost twenty years to get to know each other better. She visited my sister and me sometimes in Louisville, and we went to Columbus frequently to visit her, as well as other family members. Painfully, we never managed to build a normal mother-daughter relationship, whatever normal is. There were times when life would bring pain that only a mother's words could soothe. I did not always get the response I hoped for, but it was comforting to still have a mother to call.

After my mom's funeral, her sister, Aunt Linda, had us go to our mom's apartment to get a few items for memorabilia. I got an artificial plant that still sits in my bathroom, a small plaque that says *Don't Sweat the Small Stuff*, and her Bible. It took a few years after her death for me to really go through her Bible. When I did, I laughed, I cried, and I saw a side of her that I never knew when she was alive.

One of the things that grabbed my immediate attention as I perused her Bible was how she constantly prayed for all her children and our families; there were handwritten prayers throughout. This made me feel special, genuinely cared for. She hadn't forgotten about us. We did matter! Tucked away inside the Bible, she also had a probation letter, envelopes from Grandma Leila and my sister Neki from when they sent her money, and a receipt from paying off her furniture.

To me, the item that shone brightest was the letter she wrote to God about her addiction. I've never read anything more powerful and beautiful. She poured her heart out to God, asking him to take her addiction away so she could be the person He created her to be.

I'll never forget the day I read that letter. It unleashed

compassion for my mother that I would've sworn I never had. Up until that point, all I knew was that my mother didn't raise me, she didn't want me, and she chose a life of crime and drugs over me. In that moment and forevermore, any negative stories I was ever told or told myself about my mother instantly didn't matter. That letter showed me that my mother was human, she was broken, she wanted healing, she wanted to be happy, she wanted a relationship with her children, and she wanted to be loved. I believe that her soul is at peace and she has happiness and joy that this world could not give her.

My father, on the other hand, is now deceased, but was alive when I wrote this chapter. At that time, his whereabouts were unknown. Interestingly enough, when my father was sober or not incarcerated, similar to my grandfather, you wouldn't hear much out of him. I didn't see much of my father growing up. Neither did I want to see him, because, like every devastating hurricane, he would always bring violence and drama that would leave its victims with life-changing, lasting effects. He was feared by many. At family gatherings, I remember how grown men would either leave or tense up at the sight of him. When I did have contact with him, I noticed that, strangely, he still had a heart and cared deeply for his family. One of the fondest memories of my father was how every year, usually from prison, he would send my sister and me a birthday card. He had a broad vocabulary and wrote poetically.

After letting go of years of resentment, anger, and pain, especially after my mother passed, I held on to a glimmer of hope that my father and I could build a relationship. This hope was inspired after I graduated from graduate school. Somehow, my father heard about it and reached out to me. Being the charming, charismatic man (that he thought he was), he thought it was only fitting that a father should buy his daughter her first set of pearls, and he did. He called me one day and asked if I could meet him because he wanted to give me a graduation gift.

Believing that people can change and everyone deserves another chance, I obliged. I met him at a nice jewelry store on 4th Street in downtown Louisville, and he bought me my first and only real pearl necklace. Oh, how he lit up! He was so proud, telling everybody in the store that he was buying his daughter her first set of pearls for graduating with a master's degree. I have to admit, I was proud too. Just for a moment, I felt like a daddy's girl.

We remained cordial for a few months. We didn't talk often, but I was still receptive to him texting or calling from time to time. However, some good things do come to an end. Shortly afterward, my oldest daughter, Jessie, and my sister, Neki, called to tell me that he said some unrepeatable, unthinkable, incomprehensible words to Jessie. What a setback! Any chance for a father-daughter relationship was now no more. We wouldn't speak again for years, until one day when he saw me drive by as I was headed to a celebratory event for a friend.

As I sat in my car anxiously waiting for my friend Dana to arrive, I stared at what appeared to be a silhouette of my father, wearing a suit from the seventies, staggering around drunk as he proceeded to walk into the African American Heritage

Center. To my unpleasant surprise, once my friend, her family, and I made it inside, I saw my disheveled father sitting at one of the tables, drinking punch as if he had purchased a ticket to attend this semiformal event. Who was collecting tickets? Who let him in?

Begrudgingly, I walked over to his table in fear that if I didn't, he would make a scene. As usual, the conversation was brief. He stated that he thought I was getting an award and wanted to come and celebrate with me. I don't know why he assumed I was getting an award, but he did. Nervous, embarrassed, and not knowing what would happen next, I was mentally preparing to leave the event before it started. As always, God must've been shining down on me, because as I stood in the buffet line, contemplating my exit, my dad walked over to me, kissed me on the cheek, said "I love you, darling," and left. Whew! Talk about dodging a bullet.

Despite some of the negative things I've shared about my parents, there are parts of my identity that I get from them that I'm proud of. For example, I get my witty personality and sense of humor from my mother and maternal grandmother. Most people can never tell when I'm joking because, with a serious face, I will say or ask something random and bizarre for a shock effect. I enjoy making people laugh and smile. At my mother's funeral, I also heard stories of how caring, generous, and thoughtful she was, and I would like to think that I was blessed with some of those characteristics as well. As far as my dad, we both share a love for writing, poetic language, and sweets. He passed his sweet tooth to me. I guess you could say that I get my courage and determination from both of my parents. Talk about fearless! They were each a force to be reckoned with.

The good, the bad, and the ugly; that's my DNA.

Moment of Reflection

1. What are some of the characteristics of your biological or adopted parents?

    _____

2. Describe your immediate and extended family.

    _____

3. What role has DNA played in shaping your identity? Does it strengthen it or make it complex?

    _____

4. In what ways have your genetics influenced how you show up as a leader?

    _____

5. Does your DNA make it harder or easier for you to lead out of authenticity?

    _____

I want you to get a visual of an authentic leader in your mind. Then read each word, and if you think it's a characteristic of an authentic leader, respond *true*. If not, respond *false*.

1. Narcissism (it's all about me, me, me):

    _____

2. Self-awareness (know thyself):

    _____

3. Relational (leads with their heart):

    _____

4. Autocratic (desires total control over decision-making):

    _____

5. Transparency (honest and genuine):

    _____

6. Moral/ethical code (does the right thing):

    _____

7. Charming/charismatic (likable):

    _____

8. Fair (solicits opposing viewpoints and considers all options):

    _____

Answers: 1. F   2. T   3. T   4. F   5. T   6. T   7. F   8. T

What did we learn from this activity about how we would typically define an authentic leader? Let's look at number seven, for example. Some of you might have put true next to charming and charismatic as authentic leadership characteristics, but others may consider it to be deceitful. This is not to imply that everyone who is charming isn't who they appear to be, but for the purpose of our activity, it is false. The goal is to get you to start looking beneath the surface—beyond the mask—to see a person's character and not just what they're projecting in order to be liked.

During the previous activity, you responded based on the characteristics of authentic leaders in general. Now focus on how those characteristics apply to you.

1. What characteristics of an authentic leader come naturally to you? Which ones do you have to work on?

    _____

    _____

2. Think of ways you can use your natural, authentic leadership characteristics to inspire others that you lead to embrace their true identity and lead out of authenticity:

    _____

    _____

Need more space? Turn to page 42.

Reflections

Pillar III: Identity

If I didn't define myself for myself, I
would be crunched into other people's
fantasies for me and eaten alive.
—Audre Lorde

The third pillar is to be true to yourself. The dictionary defines identity as "the state or fact of remaining the same one or ones, as under varying aspects or conditions, or the condition of being oneself or itself, and not another." A persona is the aspect of someone's character that is presented to or perceived by others. *Persona* in Latin means "mask," a character played by an actor. Why is it that we often meet a person's persona instead of their true self? This pillar will challenge you to remove your mask(s) and embrace your true identity.

Why do we mask who we are? Could it be out of fear that if people really knew our true identity, they might not accept us? Or maybe it's not that deep. What if some of us consciously or subconsciously create personas based on people we respect or admire? Before we get deep into mirroring someone's identity, think about someone's sense of fashion that you admire. You simply like how they dress and find yourself emulating their style. Didn't some wise person once say that "Imitation is the sincerest form of flattery"?

Growing up, there was a show called *Melrose Place*, and I loved how one of the main characters, Heather Locklear, dressed. She had a classy yet sexy style that I admired. In one particular episode, she wore a baby blue pantsuit that would eventually become my signature look. When I started working more professional jobs, I would wear crop pants with fitted blazer jackets and a camisole or a white button-down shirt underneath. Over time, I wasn't known for having Heather Locklear's look; we had no other physical resemblances and no one knew where my inspiration came from, but I was known for wearing blazer jackets. Not only was this a fashion statement for me, but it helped bring less attention to my behind.

Emulating someone's style of fashion is just one way you create a public persona. Another could be aspiring to be like the characters that people play on TV, if not like your role models in real life. If you had asked me what I wanted to be when I grew up, I would have said an attorney. Growing up, one of the shows I used to watch with Grandma was *Perry Mason*, a show about a defense attorney portrayed by Raymond Burr. Perry Mason was a kick-ass lawyer who primarily represented people who were falsely accused, but he was known for drawing out the real criminal on the witness stand. Oh, how I admired him! I was so inspired that when I graduated from high school, I majored in pre-law when I enrolled in college. Eventually, I would discover that path wasn't for me, but the point I'm making is that it's possible that my public persona(s) were influenced by the people whom I watched on TV.

The mask you wear doesn't matter as much as why you mask or create a persona. If it's out of fear of rejection, I challenge you—as I've challenged myself—to take the mask off. Once we do, I believe we'll discover that we have a lot more in common than differences.

For example, who can't relate to that uncle who shows up to family events so drunk that his words slur and the only thing keeping his balance is his arm around your shoulder? No? What about that younger sibling or cousin who wanted to follow you everywhere you went when you were kids, and you were told that you couldn't go to the store, your friend's house, or the party unless you took him or her with you? No? What about the family member who squanders all their money, then asks you to borrow the money to pay a bill before it gets cut off? But don't you dare ask specific questions about what the money is for because they'll either become defensive or tell you "Just forget it, then!" Never happened to you? Perhaps that family member is you. Maybe you were the kid who couldn't afford name-brand clothes or shoes, so you got teased at school.

Okay, for argument's sake, let's say none of these resonate with you. You get the point. Everybody has something about themselves or their family that causes shame or doesn't fit into what's an acceptable societal norm. However, what you will discover with age, confidence, and maturity is that none of those things define you.

Sorrowfully, it's not just our environment and DNA that make us put on a mask. It's our personal shame and how we view ourselves based on our past, current circumstances, flaws, or mistakes. In our Western culture, we love rags-to-riches stories and humble beginnings. The sins of your family are forgiven, and you're admired and respected for overcoming disadvantaged experiences. However, when we are not as confident as we appear, don't feel smart enough, or commit a cardinal sin, we create a persona that only reflects the most flattering parts of ourselves. Then, when someone we admire and respect tries to get close to us, we withdraw and mask those qualities that we think others will use to judge us, unaware that we are most attractive and appealing to others when our guards are down and we show up as our authentic selves.

Think about a time when you were most like yourself. Was your laugh a bit obnoxious? Did you show all thirty-two teeth? Maybe you laughed until you cried, but it was at the wrong place and wrong time. It just so happens that you catch up with old friends and family at funerals. Or maybe you took a cheap shot at humor, and nobody else in the room got it except the other dork. Crickets!

The one thing all these examples have in common is the freedom of not taking yourself too seriously. Some of us don't need to drink or be a comedian to laugh or make others laugh—there's a chemical that our body releases called dopamine, which gives us a natural high. You're not controlled by outside forces or influences telling you what's acceptable behavior or not.

So, next time you meet someone, be courageous and introduce them to the real *you*. I'm confident that they won't only like you, but you might even make a friend in the end. When we allow ourselves to be vulnerable and human enough to laugh at ourselves, it gives others permission to show up in their true identity as well.

Moment of Reflection

How do you identify?

What's the first thing that just came to your mind? Your race? Your gender? Your age? Your size? Your socioeconomic status? Your religious affiliation or lack thereof? Your sexual orientation? Your job?

Pause. Take a moment to process this question. The first thing that came to your mind is how you truly see yourself. Positive or negative, it's what you believe to be true about you. Once you think a little harder, you'll start adding things to your list.

It's important to pause and ask yourself how you identify, because it explains how you show up. For example, the first time I was asked this question, I was attending a meeting at a restaurant called The Table. "The Table is a non-profit, social entrepreneurship that serves locally grown, fresh food and operates under a pay-what-you-can model." We were meeting there monthly to discuss how the church should address social justice issues. I explained the setting because as I reflect back, I believe it influenced how I responded to the question. Being in an environment with other believers and down-to-earth people of the community, created a space of vulnerability on a personal level. Whereas if I was asked that question in a corporate or professional setting, my brain probably would have taken me in a different direction regarding my identity. All that said, I responded, "I identify as Christian, Black, female, mother, and wife."

Look at the words I used. Although I'm a consultant who coaches and teaches leadership skills to teams and leaders,

I didn't mention my role or profession. I'm also passionate about women's empowerment and at-risk youth and young adults, but I did not mention that. I responded truthly to the question based on what I thought was applicable to that audience. Do you think my response would have been different if I was at work? It's a good chance it would have, but it shouldn't. A friend and a former book coach told me that "You're a whole person." In other words, your identity doesn't change based on your audience, the service/product you're offering, or the environment you're in.

When I initially started writing my manuscript, I didn't have a target audience in mind. All I knew was that I wanted to use my life's journey of struggling with embracing my identity to encourage others who are struggling with similar identity issues to embrace their true identity and stop trying to fit into what we think people want us to be. But what started as a memoir, which if I decided to publish would be found in a self-help section, was later revised to include application so that the book could be found in the self-help or business genres for leaders. This would allow the book to have further reach. And although I was still working in corporate America when I started writing this book, I had aspirations to become an independent consultant as an entrepreneur. Informed by my skill sets and areas of focus, I came up with the draft title: Cohort Leadership Coach and Team Advocate for my company's name. But as I continued to work on branding for the business and becoming an author, I thought I had to come up with two different business and marketing strategies. I was reminded that it's all products or services that I will offer. So when people go to my website, they can order a book and/or request my other services; they're not mutually exclusive.

Maybe you're like I was. You're an entrepreneur or work a day job, but you have a passion for a certain social group or a cause such as human or animal rights, legislation, Little League sports, environmentalism, or homelessness, to name a few. You tell yourself, "I'll go to the office, factory, restaurant, or school and work to earn a paycheck, and I'll do what I love to do—what I'm passionate about—in my spare time."

Why can't we do both? It's interesting how I couldn't connect the dots of how writing a book for leaders encouraging them to lead out of authenticity was no different than going to work in corporate America every day, encouraging leaders in my training and coaching sessions to always be true to themselves. Personally or professionally, I've been given a gift to encourage others. The book is just a resource used to encourage people. In corporate America or as an independent consultant, I'm the resource. The point I'm making is that no matter the environment we're in, we still have the same gifts and passions, so use them at work, at home, or in everyday casual interactions. You may never get the opportunity to get paid to do what you're most passionate about, so use your gifts and passions in every environment you grace with your presence. You are you wherever you go, so your identity or message shouldn't change—that's what leading out of authenticity is all about.

I'm often quoted as saying, "Growing up, I'm sure you never said, 'I want to work in a call center when I grow up.'"

Some leaders may have had aspirations to work in corporate America, but not in their specific role or department. How you see yourself and where you think you should be in life affects how you show up. If you always had a dream of becoming an astronaut, microbiologist, cardiologist, doctor, artist, or lawyer and you're working in a call center, factory, or restaurant, it will shape your identity, self-worth, and what you believe you are capable of.

Therefore, I challenge leaders in my training and coaching sessions to use the same gifts and talents they use when doing things they're passionate about or aspire to do in their current role until they can do it to make a living. The reality is that most people don't do that "thing" that they've always dreamed of, but it doesn't mean that you can't still tap into your purpose. Here are three scenarios that may be of benefit to you.

Scenario 1: You're a supervisor in a call center, managing a team of customer care representatives. You love nature and have a passion for improving the environment. Working at Yellowstone or Yosemite National Parks would be a dream come true for you. You're in your late thirties or early forties and can't see how it would be possible, because you have two teenagers actively involved in expensive extracurricular activities, a pet that isn't inexpensive to care for, and a mortgage (among other bills) to pay. How are you going to be able to pursue your dream job that would allow you to enjoy nature and help improve the environment?

Glad you asked. Why not start right at home? Start a garden, which will allow you to "work" in nature. Then, being true to your authentic self, go green! Reduce the amount of paper and plastics you use and recycle at home and work. You can also use your influence as a leader to share ideas on how to improve the environment. Then set up challenges and give incentives to motivate other people to reduce the amount of paper and plastics they use, reduce how much water they use, and recycle items. My hope for you is that if you never get to work at a national park, or until you do, you'll use your gifts, talents, and influence to do the things you're most passionate about.

Scenario 2: You're a school teacher who appreciates beauty and art. An ideal job for you would be painting people, places, and things that are near and dear to your heart and selling them at local art galleries. It's not about the profit for you—adding beauty to the world, especially people's homes, would be enough.

However, while you were growing up, your parents, a school counselor, or maybe society drilled into your head that you should choose a profession that pays a lot of money. Even in *Becoming*, Michelle Obama shares that once she finally got the courage to tell her mother that she was unhappy being a lawyer, her mother responded, "Make money now and be happy later." As the story goes, being the responsible, sensible, and logical person that you are, you went to college, got a degree in education, and became one of the best school teachers in your district. You're admired by many and have definitely made a difference in the world. Nonetheless, your heart is always drawn back to your love and appreciation for art. What do you do?

Unlike my advice in the previous scenario, it's slightly different for you. What I'm not going to say is that you need to teach art. Yes, you're a school teacher who is also a gifted artist, and logically, it might even make sense for you to teach art. Are you curious why that's not what I'm going to encourage you to do?

There are two types of people: those who do and those who teach. You have to determine which one you are. Can you do both? Sure! But it'll be less challenging and more fulfilling to focus on one. For example, I love to write and edit, but if I attempt to do both at the same time, it's too taxing. This can cause me to feel overwhelmed and make me give up on my project. However, if I write and hire an editor or proofread/edit someone else's work, it will be much more fulfilling to me, and I'll preserve the energy needed to focus on my passion.

Not in all cases, but if you do what you're passionate about in a profession that you're not crazy about, you could run the risk of burnout. So continue to teach whatever subject you're teaching, even if it is art, but in your spare time, paint what you're passionate about and enter your pieces into art shows. Don't lose your dream of becoming the next Picasso.

Scenario 3: You work in IT and have always wanted to be a Little League coach. You played sports growing up and it helped build up your confidence and social skills, so as an adult, you would like to give back to your community by being a coach.

However, you have a growing family and are adjusting to your newlywed being a stay-at-home mom. You've been struggling to find a position locally that pays your desired salary, so you sign a contract that pays well but requires you to travel a lot. Your new wife is happy, the family is well cared for, and you have financial security. You have finally reached the peak of Maslow's hierarchy of needs, self-actualization, based on how others describe the American dream. There's a silenced voice inside of you that wants to scream, "What about me?" but you dare not let your resentment be heard aloud. Not at the risk of appearing to be selfish and ungrateful. Unfortunately, just because you don't share your dream doesn't make your longing to coach a Little League team go away. But with your travel schedule, how will this ever happen?

Be encouraged, my friend. Continue to apply for jobs in your surrounding area. Save, save, save money for your emergency fund, and if your schedule permits, volunteer or teach others the things you're most passionate about for free. For example, as you desire to coach but can't just yet, find a coach who could use a mentor—you. Every good leader needs a good coach. In addition, when you're on the road alone, in between solving technical problems, you could write blogs giving tools and tips on effective coaching and/or hold weekly one-hour virtual coaching sessions with coaches or aspiring coaches to help develop their skills and boost their self-esteem. Leading out of your authenticity, focusing on your passions, even if you're not in the role yourself or getting paid for mentoring or teaching others, will give you a sense of purpose and sustain you until your dream of becoming a Little League coach comes true.

Regardless of the scenarios, the advice is to be practical about your life circumstances. As such, I encourage you to carve out time to dedicate to your passions and not give up on them. Your passions and dreams are a part of your identity, so when you allow them to come alive, it propels you one step closer to leading out of authenticity. Maybe none of these scenarios resonate with you, but I want you to stay tuned because I'm confident that you will find something in this book that will inspire you to lead out of authenticity and be your best self. Let's go back to my original question: *How do you identify?* It is important for you to know who you are, what you have to offer, and why nobody else can do what you do like you. You were created with a unique personality, specific gifts, talents, and passions to make a difference in the world that no one else can do except you. It's one thing for me to see it in you, but it's more important that you see it in yourself and believe it! Remember that your passion and the work you get paid to do don't have to be mutually exclusive.

Embracing your true identity and all its complexities will allow people to get the best of you. Now, no matter what environment I'm in, the next time someone asks me, "How do you identify?" I'm going to say: "I identify as a woman of faith who believes that all people have a purpose, and my purpose is to lead out of authenticity and inspire others to do the same."

Pillar IV: Personality

You have to decide who you are and force the
world to deal with you, not with its idea of you.
—James Baldwin

Many philosophers and researchers believe that human beings are made up of at least four personality types, with everyone having a trace of each one, but one or two may be more prevalent or dominant than others. There are dozens of personality assessments with their own interpretations. For example, according to Hippocrates, a person's personality can be characterized as sanguine, choleric, phlegmatic, or melancholic. Someone with a sanguine personality is known to be harmonious and sociable. Someone who is choleric has an ambitious, take-charge type of personality, while phlegmatic personality types are passive and easygoing. Someone who is melancholic is known to be analytical and logical.

One of the courses I'm certified to facilitate is called Real Colors. This is not the same as True Colors, a similar but different assessment that some of you may be familiar with. Real Colors uses a four-color personality assessment to help individuals identify their personality type. From my experience, most people who have taken the Real Colors assessment identify with a dominant personality type and agree that their results best describe them, but, like any assessment, it's not cookie-cutter. Therefore, there are people who identify with more than one personality type. If you wish to learn more about Real Colors, you can go to their website realcolors.org or contact me directly if you wish to take an assessment. My contact information is in the back of the book.

There is a plethora of personality assessments that you can take, and although I find them to be useful to better understand yourself and others and how to effectively communicate, there's nobody who knows you like you do. The problem is that some people have been masking or wearing a persona for so long, they don't know who they are. If this is you, you're right where you need to be: reading a book that will help you self-discover. Pillar IV is to help you embrace your personality and no longer entertain the voice in your head or other people telling you what you should be. Through your personality, people really get to know the uniqueness of you—good and bad.

The words "simply complex" in the book title come before "leading out of authenticity" because being authentic may sound simple but can be messy and complex. "Simply complex" also best describes my personality. Has anyone ever asked you "What do you love about yourself?" and you struggled to answer (if you ever came up with an answer)? But if asked, "Tell me something you don't like about yourself or would change," your mouth becomes a bottomless pit. Does it marvel you that the brain tends to hold onto negativity longer than positivity?

In part, it could be due to how our brains are wired for fight or flight. It doesn't distinguish the difference between physical and emotional pain. One of the main functions of the amygdala is to store emotions, especially those for survival. Therefore, if a person is under stress or fearful too long, the brain can release a chemical called cortisol that will contribute to holding on to negativity even longer. Even if one argues the science behind this, what about the role society plays in how we view ourselves?

In our Western culture, we're taught that humility is a virtue, yet we tell our kids that they can be whatever they want to be. We encourage them to be their best and strive to be number one. But when they do, we accuse them of being arrogant. This is often seen in sports when a team or an individual are consistent winners. You will start to hear people say, "They win all the time—I'm going for the underdog." There's nothing wrong with wanting to see the underdog win, but why can't we still applaud winners for their achievement? What a contradictory message we send when we encourage people to have confidence and believe in themselves but call them arrogant when they do.

I was raised to be humble yet confident. But admittedly, I often play myself down around people who tend to take jabs at me or if I sense that they have low confidence. Painfully, the jabs are typically from people who I would least expect it from, such as friends or extended family (my immediate family is very supportive of me) who are demeaning, as if it were their job to keep me in my place. You may know people who say complimentary things about you as long as you don't agree with their compliment or confidently say thank you. If you do, they'll say something to belittle you or keep you in your place.

One time, when I facilitated a strategy meeting for the vice president of our department, she later sent an email and copied my boss, stating what a good job I did. Later that day, I ran into my boss, and he said, "That was really nice of our vice president to send you a compliment, because she don't give them out easily." In response, I said, "I know; how nice, I was really surprised." But before a glimpse of a smile could appear on my face, my boss said, "Don't let it go to your head—just as fast as someone can go up, they can fall down."

What message do you think this sent to me? Never acknowledge a compliment or say anything nice about myself in front of my boss. Again, he could tell me that I was smart, talented, even good enough, but other interactions like the one aforementioned taught me early on that I couldn't fully be authentically who I was created to be, at least not around him.

Having these types of people in my life has definitely caused my confidence to waver at times, but over the years, I've done a good job of disassociating from people who try to control my level of confidence and self-worth. If you can relate, I want to encourage you to surround yourself with people who are secure in who they are, so that you can be confident in who *you* are, not playing yourself small to fit in. This means if you have an infectious personality that people are drawn to, let your light shine.

It breaks my heart when I hear people say that they were always told they were never going to be anything. In part, because I believe that everyone has a purpose, but even given my disadvantaged background, I can't recall anyone ever telling me that. On the contrary, especially when I was a child, I remember adults speaking words of encouragement and telling me how much they believed in me. Although I rarely sensed pity, I'm very grateful and appreciative. This could support my underdog theory that people like to root for those who come from humble beginnings. Who knows? Regardless, never underestimate the power of someone believing in you. Sure, you should have confidence and believe in yourself, but I believe that a lot of my drive to "make it" was because I had people who believed in me.

Educationally, my grandmother and uncles had very high expectations of us kids. It was unacceptable to bring home any grade less than a B. Not very many Bs were on my report card, which inadvertently raised the standard. Moreover, if I did earn a C or lower, I knew a strict punishment would be enforced. On one occasion, in elementary school, I tried to forge my grandma's signature on my report card, but she soon found out because I spelled Margaret wrong. As a result, not only was I disciplined at school and by my grandmother but also when my uncle Charles came over and asked to see my report card, I got in trouble again. My uncle Wilbur, on the other hand, was highly intelligent, but the lenient uncle who often took a different approach. If we got a bad grade, he would let us come to his home to hang out and have fun, but before we left, he would quiz us on history or make us read the encyclopedia. Everyone in my family played a different role in Neki's and my development, but they all held us accountable.

So, what does how people saw me or the expectations they had of me have to do with my personality? It wasn't until I became an adult—more specifically, when I started taking assessments—that I discovered that my dominant personality type is a balance of sanguine and analytical, which is one of the reasons I identify as "simply complex." I believe it was the qualities associated with the dominant parts of my personality that allowed adults to see in me as a child what I didn't see in myself.

As a child, I didn't see it. And as an adult, I couldn't accept it, but I can now reflect and appreciate it. I remember when one of my teachers, Ms. Patrick, found out that I was pregnant. She came to my house to encourage me to put my unborn child up for adoption because she believed that I had a bright future ahead of me.

Back then, I couldn't receive that as positive feedback. At the first feeling of my child inside of me, I knew that I could never let him go, so to hear someone present an alternative to me only infuriated me. It would take at least thirty years to realize just how much potential she must've seen in me. Up until this point, Ms. Patrick was merely an English teacher. We had no connection or relationship for her to make a personal visit to my home.

There was another occasion when I was a young adult working in corporate America that an older colleague pulled me aside to tell me that someone I considered a friend wasn't a friend to me. Being the relational person I am, friendships mean everything to me. Therefore, for her to speak those dreadful words that I had been suppressing in willful disbelief (for the sake of the friendship) was not easily received.

As such, to further prove her argument, she went on to say that "She's jealous of you."

I quickly retorted, "Jealous of what? She's prettier than me. She gets more attention than me and she clearly has nicer things than I do."

The lady refuted my argument. "It has nothing to do with what you have or how you look—she's jealous of what you have inside. You have a light that draws people to you and because she doesn't have it, I notice how she tries to dim your light."

I wish I could tell you that the friendship ended then, but it didn't. Many years would pass before I could disassociate from someone whom I loved dearly, but secretly I always knew that her intentions were never pure with me.

One of the benefits of personality assessments is not only to tell you who you are but to also help you better "understand" who you are. And, if you're interested, they help you better understand other people. To that end, at the beginning of this chapter, remember when I said there were four personality types? I'm going to go over the four main types of personalities that researchers and philosophers believe we have to help you identify yours, in case you don't know or need further clarification. In addition, I'll continue to share parts of my personal story to encourage you to accept and embrace the personality that makes you, you.

My Personality Type Analysis

Reader, I'm going to provide an in-depth analysis of my personality type in hopes that, through my exploration, it encourages you to do the same.

If I had to label the part of my personality that people probably gravitate to, it would be sanguine. People with a sanguine type of personality are typically optimistic, cheerful, and like harmony. But according to Myers and Briggs, I'm an ENFJ (extroverted, intuitive, feeling, and judgment), which is a lot deeper than just being optimistic, cheerful, and harmonious. ENFJs are known as protagonists because we are passionate, effortlessly see the best in others, and will stop at no expense, emotionally or otherwise, to ensure you develop and pursue your true purpose.

I suppose this is what this friend must have seen in me. Ironically, what she didn't see was how lonely this left me. Sure, people with my personality type get pure satisfaction in bringing out the best in others, but these relationships rarely develop into friendships. People begin to rely on ENFJs for inspiration and motivation, but due to no fault of their own, they don't have the same capacity to reciprocate in return, even if they want to. For me, this makes most connections ministry—not friendships—which is why ENFJs can be in a room full of people and still feel lonely. If I had a dollar for every time someone told me how much better they felt after talking to me, I'd be a pretty wealthy woman. This is not a humblebrag. It sounds noble to naturally put others before yourself, but what's often taken for granted with this personality type is our desire for friendships that we rarely ever attain.

In part, this is why I've always struggled with my personality type. First, I don't like how deeply I feel. There's nothing wrong with being compassionate and passionate, but not to the point that I start taking on other people's problems as my own. Second, my personality type can be emotional and a little on the sensitive side. This is probably the thing that drives others, including myself, crazy. But what I've learned to accept and have conveyed to others who love my passionate, inspiring, and optimistic side is that they have to accept the emotional and sensitive side that is inherently a part of my personality as well. What about you? Do you like your personality? Is there anything about your personality that you don't like, or do you tend to adapt to the personality of the person or people you're around to fit in?

So often, we only want to experience the more positive qualities of people, getting easily irritated by seeming character flaws. Nonetheless, the positive and negative makes you who you are, so I'm encouraging you, as I've encouraged myself, to embrace the personality that you were created with.

The other qualities that make up my dominant personality style are the honest, direct, sensible, and pragmatic sides of me. Juxtaposed with my sanguine qualities of harmony, compassion, and empathy, they can make me seem like a walking contradiction, but it's all me. Depending on the environment where you meet me, you will have a different perception of me. However, usually, your first interaction with me will more than likely be warm, friendly, and welcoming, regardless of the setting. I naturally want people to feel comfortable and know that they matter to me. But where the switch may flip for some people is when I'm handling business of any kind. No matter the warm welcome you receive from me, when I'm working on a project or faced with addressing an issue or concern, I naturally become serious, sensible, and matter-of-fact. Talk about simply complex.

A leader once told me that I can be off-putting, and I said, "Not me!" My reaction wasn't because I couldn't see it, but it was contrary to anything I had ever been told. Most people typically tell me that I'm kind and friendly. But my leader, at the time, being the wise woman that she is, knows something about me that most people with limited interactions with me don't see on the surface: When I'm focused on something or have a deadline to meet, those in my path become inconspicuous to me. Yes, this can make me off-putting, especially if most of one's interactions with me have been congenial. In addition to becoming more serious, my communication becomes more honest and direct, which is the polar opposite of the other side of my personality that is diplomatic and careful not to offend. Whew! Can anyone relate to me? If so, keep in mind that not everyone can digest such candor without a little Novocain. But for the most part, I'm told that people respect my honesty and transparency, and I can only assume that they sense my positive intent.

The next qualities of my personality are not as dominant as the others aforementioned, but they're still inherently a part of who I am. The analytical spark, logic, and curiosity that flow through me are the qualities that I probably most appreciate about my personality. These characteristics, complemented by introspection, settled my brain down long enough to write this book. Again, simply complex. You take me, this social butterfly, who loves people but will physically and emotionally withdraw from people, not needing another soul. When I tell people that I'm an introvert who operates as an extrovert, they all but call me a liar. And I completely understand why. But the truth is that as much as I enjoy talking to people on the elevator, in the grocery store, and loved ones on the phone, I equally enjoy times alone with my thoughts.

Two of my favorite pastimes are reading and writing, with a cup of coffee, of course. There was this time when I went on a much-awaited girls' trip to the Smoky Mountains in Gatlinburg—another favorite thing to do. I was asked to speak at the last minute at a special event the next weekend. Knowing that the upcoming week would be demanding, personally and professionally, the only time I would have to study and prepare would have to be some time on this girls' trip. Now, whenever I go to the mountains, I'm going to steal some "me time" to read and/or write with a scenic view. There's not much more that I can ask for, other than being surrounded by people I love and adore.

We got to our delightful chalet late Friday afternoon, and I was fully engaged with all my girls (Dana, Brig, TJ, Veronica, Jennifer, and my sister, Neki) and all the activities. Now, there's a part of my personality that I haven't explained yet, but for the purpose of this story, you'll get a glimmer of it now. For a moment, imagine seven similar yet very distinctive women. Everyone is either close to or over the age of forty, cooking or watching others cook in the kitchen. I jump onto the back of one of the ladies, who I call the yang to my ying.

Now, not everyone is going to see this side of my personality, but these women bring out the more amusing and humorous side of me. We had a blast—talking, laughing, playing games, and watching movies all night. Interestingly enough, those who know me well know that I'm not a night owl, so staying up past 10 p.m., girls' trip or not, can be a challenge for me. Nonetheless, my attitude, at least that weekend, was the adage, "I'll sleep when I'm dead." Sounds fun, right? I'm living outside of my box.

After hearing the description of my dominant personality, do you really buy that? You shouldn't. It's not that I wanted to sleep, but do you recall the point I made earlier about needing some "me time" to prepare a message for my speaking engagement? I also said that even if I didn't have to prepare a message, I still needed some "me time" to read and/or write. Let's just say that I stayed true to my authentic self, which is a great time to pause to talk about why people struggle with authenticity. Sometimes when you choose to be true to yourself, you won't be popular with others.

After cooking and eating breakfast together, we needed to decide what we were going to do for the day, keeping in mind that although it was a girls' trip, we all had individual agendas as well. Out of the seven ladies, someone wanted to go hiking, another wanted to go to the town to buy moonshine, and yours truly wanted a few hours to write. All the other ladies were open to doing whatever the majority wanted to do. Given that half were going into town for moonshine and the other half were going to the outlet mall, I didn't see me staying at the chalet to write as a disruption of our time together. Oh, on the contrary.

A couple of the ladies—interestingly enough, the two who had the strongest personal preferences, as opposed to the others, who were happy to go along with the majority, were disappointed that I wanted to stay at the chalet to write. Given that I try to be open to other people's perspectives, I can see how me staying at the chalet to write could seem antisocial because although the two groups weren't together, I was the only one who was alone.

Respectfully, however, if put in the same situation again, I would make the same decision. The reality is that I'm more adaptable and compromising than not, but when I make my mind up that I'm going to do something, I'm not easily persuaded otherwise. Thankfully, my moment of rebellion didn't ruin our trip. However, the next year, when some of us got together for a short road trip, I was served advance notice and continuously reminded that I couldn't read in the car, although I had driven my part and stayed awake for the driver while others were peacefully sleeping. This I laughed off and actually complied with the request. But when we started to plan a cruise and I was told that I couldn't go to the serenity room to read, I told my beautiful friend that enough was enough. "Just like you have a mental or written itinerary of things you'd like to do when we're not spending time together, so do I."

I'm sure you've heard that opposites attract. There's still debate about that, but I do believe that people who are different from you can bring out the best of you. Why? When you're challenged to think beyond how you typically think, act differently from how you naturally feel, and see the world through others' perspectives, it can give you the full range to meet with people on any level and truly make a difference in the world.

Conversely, I also believe that there still has to be a healthy balance. No matter your personality type, we all want somebody, anybody, to "get us." We need to find where we fit in in this gigantic world, with the least amount of opposition or rejection. Outside of my friend groups, I've been Sherlocked (one of many fans of the 2010 *Sherlock Holmes* TV series), and my youngest daughter, Dejah, is a Potterhead (one of the terms used for diehard Harry Potter fans), to name a couple of communities where one could find a sense of belonging. Do you have a group, community, sorority, or fraternity you belong to? You all may not necessarily have the same values, but you will have a special connection based on a shared interest.

I have a few different friend groups, but the thing they all have in common is that they're not favorable of the more analytical, introverted, and scrupulous side of my personality. To that end, I do us all a favor and occasionally disconnect so that they don't have to tolerate this side of me, and I can retreat in solitude where I'm free to be my authentic self. But what I would encourage you to do (as I'm in the process of doing the same) is open yourself up to attract or find someone who reminds you of you. Some would call that person a kindred spirit. The simplest definition I found in the dictionary describes a kindred spirit as a person whose interests or attitudes are similar to one's own.

The fourth and last personality type I'll explicate is the one that I least identify with: the 4-Cs, which are confident, clownlike, competitive, and courageous. This type is definitely the life of the party. I know I previously shared a moment where I got loose and jumped on Yang's back while we all gathered in the kitchen during our girls' trip. But even with that occasion, it's very unlikely that anyone would ever describe me as the life of the party. Interestingly enough, most of the friends in my inner circle are.

What's important to remember whenever you're studying personality types is that although most researchers believe that we all have a little or a lot of every quality in us, what most people are going to see or experience when interacting with us, if we're being our authentic selves, are the dominant ones. Case in point: from time to time, I tap into the 4-Cs, but unlike my dominant traits, these traits are wavering. I can be confident but easily discouraged. I can be clownlike yet boring. I can be competitive but not a sore loser. But the one that is probably the least fleeting is courage. I tend to do most things in fear, but I will do them, nonetheless. This also applies to having difficult conversations. I have some friends who always describe me as courageous, simply based on the conversations I'm willing to have. In part, I agree, but it's not just about me being courageous, it's also about the sanguine personality in me that likes harmony and peace. Back in my people-pleasing days, my friend Dana would always say, "Peace means authority." In other words, my reluctance to address conflict may have spared me an argument outwardly but disturbed my peace inwardly. Regardless of the desire for peace or not, I have to admit that courage is one of my more recently utilized higher qualities.

The only quality that is not of great importance to me in this personality type is clownlike or having fun, at least not all the time. I enjoy a good time just as much as the next person, but it's not a core value or need, and it has a lot to do with my dominant personality. More specifically, it depends on how one might define fun. I admire people who work hard then play hard, but based on my interests, this wouldn't describe me. I like to work hard, and my idea of playing hard would be retreating to the mountains or the beach with a refreshing beverage and a book. This is why so many of my friends who fall into this personality type may think I'm a little weird. That's because they are more carefree, not considering that I'm wired differently from them, so clearly something must be wrong with me.

I chuckle as I reflect on one of my favorite girls' trips. It was my dear friend Shanté's bridal shower getaway that lasted for almost a week at Chateau Élan Winery and Resort in Georgia. Talk about a blast! There were at least ten of us, at a minimum. Shanté and our other dear friend Tajna drove to the resort together and stayed in the same room. This was a different group of friends from the ones previously mentioned, but you're going to notice a reoccurring theme.

On our way to Georgia, similar to my other girls' trip, it was nothing short of incredible. We laughed, talked, shared stories, listened to good music, and even picked up Shanté's cousin, Toya, in Tennessee. Not only did she have a lovely personality, but I was also personally grateful for her because she had planned every detail of this trip, something I would typically do when traveling with family or friends. As such, we all enjoyed each other's company and had a smooth ride to Georgia.

The purpose of this trip was to party and celebrate, so our mantra became "Turn down for what." For those of you who are not familiar with this phrase, it implies that you're going to party all day and night. This came as no surprise to me because Toya, being the consummate bridal shower planner she was, had given us an itinerary in advance of all events. But being true to myself, I still took a book.

I need all my friends to understand that if we're traveling together for more than an hour, more than likely I'm going to bring a book. First, I enjoy reading, but due to having such a demanding personal and professional life, the only time I get to actually finish the entire book is when I take time off from work. The second reason is that I don't like downtime. So, being an early riser, if everyone else is still asleep, I can read, or if we just happen to get a break during the day, I'd like to read.

The latter is exactly what I did. Every morning, I would get up at least an hour and a half to two hours before my roommates and would go to the fitness center at the resort and read while walking on the treadmill. Of course, no one had a problem with what they couldn't see, but when I started to read while I waited for my turn in the shower was when they started to rib me. Okay, maybe I deserved to be teased for bringing a book on a bridal shower getaway, but hey, I have to read when I can.

The ribbing I received from two of my closest friends was justified, even welcomed, but the true comedic moment happened when I got dressed to go out for a night on the town. Just in case you got lost in the story and have forgotten the personality type I'm talking about, if you can't remember the 4-Cs, just remember that my least dominant trait of the 4-C's is clowning around and letting loose. Again, it's how one defines fun. For the sake of argument, this example will highlight letting loose. Even though I'm far from a prima donna (although I have been called that once), I like to have a classy yet sexy look, especially for a night out on the town. I also had recently lost a considerable amount of weight that enabled me to get in a dress that I had bought a while ago but couldn't fit in. In my mind, when the itinerary stated that everyone needed to wear a little black dress, on this particular night, I thought I had the perfect outfit.

On the evening that we were scheduled to go out on the town, I was the first to get dressed out of the three in our room. But surprisingly, no one commented on how I looked. Humbly speaking, this was an oddity for our group because we all were very generous with complimenting one another, so I was starting to get a little concerned about my dress. But what was unspoken with my roommates was explicitly addressed when the other ladies started to come into our room.

Going back to the chuckle I started with, I laugh when I think about how a team of ladies pulled together to get me out of what they referred to as my "church dress." You would've thought that I was on one of those makeover shows. A few ladies offered accessories. One lady donated a tank top. Another slid a swimsuit cover over my head, and thankfully, I had black leggings. Otherwise, I'm convinced they would've sent me out in some black fishnet pantyhose and heels.

Now, that was fun. A little embarrassing, but fun. Of course, I don't think that they thought I knew how to let loose and have fun, but to this day, I appreciate the genuine care that they put into making me look hot. The alternative is that they didn't have to care, and they could have let me go out thinking that I looked just fine.

I confess: out of all the qualities I've shared of the primary four personality types, clowning around is by far the one that comes the least naturally to me, but fun is the one personality trait I try to tap into the most because, like Cyndi Lauper said, "Girls just want to have fun."

It was fun for me to take you all on some of my special journeys, but what does a person's personality have to do with leading out of authenticity? Once a person accepts—even embraces—his or her personality, hopefully, they'll permit those they lead to show up as their authentic selves. They no longer have to try to be something or someone that others think they should be. No more apologizing for being too nice, too aggressive, too introverted, or overly confident. Show up and be proud of the person you were created to be.

If you're interested in learning more about who you are according to Myers and Briggs, there's a free online assessment you can take called 16Personalities. As previously stated, if you're interested in discovering your personality type according to Real Colors, you can reach out to NCTI at realcolors.org or contact me directly for a consultation to schedule a team-building session for a group in need of building trust or effectively communicating with people who are new to the team or wired up differently. Personality assessments that are taken individually, with a partner, or in a small group can be a fun way of better understanding why you think the way you do, act the way you do, or see the world through your particular lenses. In addition, your results will give you labels, terms, or language to help explain certain aspects of you that you may have struggled to put into words. This will not only be beneficial to you but also just as useful for those you interact with the most.

Pillar V: Love

Love recognizes no barriers. It jumps
hurdles, leaps fences, penetrates walls to
arrive at its destination full of hope.
—Maya Angelou

According to Harvard Health Publishing, "Whether you're hitting a tennis ball or mopping the floor, the necessary motions either originate in your core, or move through it." Recently, I had to go see an orthopedic specialist after several months of wishing away my knee pain. Thankfully, my x-rays came back normal and the doctor confirmed what I already knew but didn't want to admit: I had overused my knee from jogging on the treadmill seven days a week. Delightedly, the treatment he prescribed was to rest it and give it time to heal.

Then he went on to say that when I walk, "Tighten your core." I subconsciously put my hand on my lower abdomen to demonstrate how he had told me to walk.

To my surprise, he immediately stopped me and said, "That's not your core." After seeing my reaction, he said, "Yes, the abdominal muscles are part of your core, but I'm referring to what's called the muscular corset, located around your lower spine and hips." Did you know that?

Ah, the pillar of love is the core of authenticity. It would be impossible to lead out of authenticity without the pillar of love. Without love, there is no trust. Without love, there is no empathy. Without love, there is no respect. Without love, there is no forgiveness. Who you are at your core is shown by how you treat people. The reality is that you are going to lead people whom you don't understand because they are different from you. How do you move past these differences to get to understanding? Love. You are going to lead people whom you don't like because they represent something or someone who has caused you pain. How do you see past that? Love. We draw strength from our core.

For my knee to heal, I must know where my core is, but when it comes to love being the core of authenticity, the location doesn't matter—just lead with it. No matter your race, religion, sexual orientation, or age, the one thing we all have in common is our desire to be loved. You can always tell if someone feels loved based on how secure they are. An insecure person tends to need a lot of reaffirmation. To you, this could feel like nothing you do is ever good enough. One of the most common examples of an adult not feeling loved is how the adult was raised as a child. They could have been placed in foster care, adopted, sent to live with a family member, or neglected in their parent's care.

Let's explore the child who was given up for adoption. Adoption is the ultimate form of love, right? Someone chose you! They picked you! Usually, they spent a lot of time, money, and resources to get you. But unfortunately, a lot of children of adoption still feel abandoned and rejected.

Then there's the child whose biological parents took a test drive at parenting to see how things might work out, but when it became too demanding or drugs and partying seemed more appealing, they dropped the child off to a family member to live. Remember my story? I was told and believed that my mother brought my sister and me to Louisville to visit with our paternal grandmother and never came back to pick us up. Even if the situation didn't happen just like that, the fact remains that we never went back to live with our mother. Did I feel loved by my grandmother? Yes! I also had lots of family who loved and helped care for me. But nothing or no one can fill the void of a parent.

Another is the example of the child who was raised by both or at least one biological parent. From what I've been told, although physically present, the parent or parents could've been abusive, emotionally unavailable, or just didn't know how to love well.

Take all these emotionally or physically abandoned children who grew up longing for love and affection from the people who actually conceived them or assumed guardianship, and you'll find adults struggling with low self-esteem, lack of self-confidence, and an inferiority complex. Before you say it, of course not everyone who was abandoned or neglected falls into this category, but if we're being honest, if not ourselves, we've met people who do. This also does not take into consideration certain personality types who naturally have confidence and a high value of self. But, if not loved well, these individuals may internally suffer from low self-esteem and low self-worth, but they are able to mask it better with charisma and/or humor. However, just because someone doesn't feel loved doesn't mean they're not loved. Maybe they haven't experienced healthy or unconditional love. As a leader, if you remember nothing else in this book, cut and paste this pillar as a reminder that love is the core of leading out of authenticity.

Moment of Reflection

What's love got to do with leadership?

One of the first times I heard the word "heart" used in a corporate setting was in a train the trainer session administered by Vital Smarts (innovator in corporate training), where I was certified in a course to help people get unstuck when having a Crucial Conversation (e.g., opinions differ, high emotions and high stakes). One of my key takaways from that training was that if your heart or motives aren't pure, you won't reach a genuine outcome, even if you "win" the conversation. If you desire to lead out of authenticity, you have to have pure intentions. Winning or being right can't be your motivation.

So, what's love got to do with it? Everything. As a leader, you will lead people who don't feel loved and who could potentially poison or sabotage your team. People are more receptive to advice, constructive feedback, and instructions when they trust that the person has their best interests at heart. Whether you're a coach, teacher, mentor, parent, or manager, there will always come a time when you'll have to have a hard conversation. It lessens the blow when it's done in love.

I'm not saying you have to go around saying "I love you" or hugging everyone. Some people do that, which is fine as long as it's not an ethics violation or a violation of personal space. However, there's a lot of people who aren't wired that way. If this is you, no worries.

So, how is leading with love done in practice? Love is an action word. Leading with love is about creating a culture that shows that you're invested and genuinely care. Your actions will go much further than your words.

Five Love Actions

If you're curious about how to create a culture where people feel loved and cared for, here are five actions you can do immediately.

1. Know everyone by their name or their preferred name, know how to pronounce it, and use it.

2. Ask questions about their interests, family, hobbies, and passions.

3. Make time and be present.

4. Take time to build relationships.

5. Start with a clean slate every day.

Action #1: In the book *How to Win Friends and Influence People,* Dale Carnegie talks about the power of using someone's name. It's so powerful that clever or manipulative people may choose to use name (or not) to get their desired response from you. For example, since we're on the topic of love, the next time you're wondering if someone is crushing on you, pay attention to if they never use your name when addressing you or if they tend to overuse your name. I'm not sure why the former happens, but from my observation, when someone likes you, saying your name seems too intimate so they'll try to communicate without it. Others will overuse your name, thinking it'll make you feel special. I believe both can be done subconsciously.

Even if you've never experienced "the name thing" romantically, have you ever worked with the public? If yes, can you recall saying the customers' names repeatedly, especially if you were trying to resolve an issue to help keep them calm? Typically, this would be more formal, so you would probably use their last name with a prefix.

Occasionally, you run into someone that you met once at a meeting, friend's house, or party and see them out and they say, "Hello, (insert your name)!" Does that not make you feel special? Maybe you pause and think, "They actually remembered my name."

No matter how big your team is or who your top performers are, if you want to create a culture where everyone has a sense of belonging, use people's names!

Action #2: If using someone's name makes them feel special, how much more special do you think it would make them feel if you asked about their family, hobbies, passions, and interests? Talk about feeling like you're invested! In my current role as a consultant and coach, if time permits, I open every session by asking about the participant as a person. Before talking about what's been going on at work, I ask about family, pets, hobbies, and passions.

Here's a tip: In my eight-week coaching sessions, I inform them that I like to take notes. I used to do the same thing when I was a supervisor and had one-on-ones with my associates. Realistically, even if you have a great memory, if you have a big team, you may not remember every intricate detail that everyone shares; writing it down will help you recall it in a later interaction. What you're trying to accomplish by writing it down is being able to reference the wedding they attended, the book they're writing, their child's basketball tournament, or their pet's name. Of course, you're not going to read from an index card or sticky note. The goal of Actions 1 and 2 is to start building a connection.

Action #3: Have you ever heard the adage, "People will forget what you say and what you do, but they'll never forget how you make them feel"? It's true. Every interaction isn't about what's said or not said. Sometimes it's about making time and being present.

How many times have you had a one-on-one with a leader that one or both of you decided to skip because you didn't have any updates? I know I'm guilty of it, but I also know that I've walked away motivated and re-energized from some of those meetings where very little was said, but my leader was there for me. More importantly, it mattered to me that he/she cleared their calendar and kept time set aside for me. It's okay to even have awkward silence. Don't feel that you need to fill the air with words. There's something refreshing about just being present. That time is allotted for you and those you lead to disconnect from the hustle and recharge. *Make* time and be present!

Action #4: Not that you have to do these actions in any particular order, but let's say that the first three actions are about building connections. Guess what's going to happen next? Almost effortlessly, you will start to naturally build a relationship. Trust is earned, not given. Building a relationship should be no different. Leaders of new and existing teams, no one has a reason to trust you with their career, emotions, ideas, or passions until you've earned it. How do you earn trust?

Develop a solid relationship built out of transparency, honesty, and integrity, and trust will happen over time. Rome wasn't built in a day and neither are genuine, long-lasting relationships. I'm not saying that you can't instantly connect with someone, but the difference between a connection and a relationship is the time it will last. I can't count the number of connections that I've made with people personally and professionally throughout my career that ended once that "thing," event, season, or project ended. However, the *relationships* that I've built I still have today. The ones that were real, we never had to define it—it just was.

Most of us think more highly of ourselves than we should. You know yourself to be kind, generous, thoughtful, and compassionate. Why wouldn't someone immediately trust you or instantly have a relationship with you? Nobody knows you like you know you. But if you're anything like me, sometimes I don't even trust myself to make unbiased decisions and have pure motives. How can I expect someone I've just met to think so highly of me?

It doesn't matter if you're a leader in your home, church, work, school, or sports team, nobody cares about you saying "I love you" if your actions don't align with your words. We are flawed people, even as leaders, and we're going to get it wrong more than we get it right. But if you establish a strong relationship with those you lead, they'll be a lot more forgiving and understanding of your indiscretions.

Action #5: Knowing that everyone has their full share of mistakes and shortcomings, how reassuring and reaffirming would it be to start each day with a clean slate? Think about how you feel when you're having an argument or disagreement with someone and they bring up something that you thought you were forgiven for years ago.

I didn't say "yesterday." No, some people won't bring up your most recent offense. They'll go back to something from long ago that you were thinking had been resolved. Imagine waking up every day reminded of all the mistakes and poor decisions you made the day before? *Every day.* Disturbingly, this is what a lot of leaders do without ever saying a word. It's called silent guilt.

Silent guilt can take on many forms. It can be as subtle as not responding when someone calls in, calls out sick, or complains to you about what others on the team are doing, which can be a tactic to discourage you from doing the same thing(s). Silent guilt is also treating an employee differently to manipulate or control the environment or the outcome of a situation.

Earlier in my career, I was highly recommended and hired for a position that I was qualified for. To embellish, I almost said "highly qualified," but that would be a stretch. The point is, it was a promotion, not a lateral move, so when I joined the team, there were high expectations of me. So high, I was assigned three major accounts, even as the newbie. Starting out, I was honored that they had so much faith in me, and I had no problem keeping up.

Unfortunately, sooner rather than later, I gradually started to drown. Coming so highly recommended, I didn't want them to regret their decision, and neither did I want to appear incompetent. As a result, I didn't ask for help. I've always been determined, so even if it required longer hours, I would keep up.

With this can-do attitude, I did keep up, until a mistake was found on a monthly report that I submitted to one of my high-profile clients. To be clear, this wasn't rocket science, nor would the mistake be a matter of life or death. Nonetheless, there was zero margin for error, especially with this client.

Given I've shared a lot of what most would perceive as embarrassing things with you, there are not many things in life that I regret or feel ashamed of. But how I was treated on a daily basis after this mistake started to make me self-conscious. I didn't stay in that role much longer. Nothing was directly stated, but I was handled as though I was incompetent. I realized that the perception of me wasn't going to change, at least not anytime soon after that incident. Truthfully, we all made mistakes, starting with me not asking for help and them assigning one person to three of their major accounts without support. Without redemption or a clean slate, I was never going to be able to work back up to the standard of expertise they hired me for. Having such a strong work ethic and high expectations of myself, it was time for me to rebrand myself. I left.

Once I left, still having a good relationship with my colleagues and director, I was told that they hired three people to replace me. I shared that story to show you the impact of not allowing people to make a mistake and to start each day with a clean slate.

You ask, what's love got to do with it? It has to do with your bottom line, your profit. A return on your investment. Employee engagement drives a sense of belonging, which leads to employee satisfaction and retention. Done well, it will set you apart from your competitors. If the word "love" is too mushy for you, change it to "motives" or "intentions." But if you're going to lead out of authenticity and build a high-performing team, you have to show that you have a heart.

Reflections

Pillar VI: Stand up!

There is only one duty, only one safe course,
and that is to try to be right and not to fear
to do or say what you believe to be right.
—Winston Churchill

The pillar Stand Up shows you what you're made of. It's easy for most people to stand up for the people they love, a cause they believe in, or to get what they want. I know parents who will stand up to you for protecting them after they've been disrespected by their child. I know women who will stand up for their spouses, even if they catch them in the act. To stand up for another person really isn't about them. It's not even about your passion or love toward them. It's about how you choose to outwardly express your loyalty, despite internal disappointment or pain. The pillar Stand Up is key to building trust, which is needed to lead out of authenticity. The people you lead will show up for you when they know that you've got their back.

Except for books such as *The Five Dysfunctions of a Team* by Patrick Lencioni and *Leadership and Self-Deception* by The Arbinger Institute, I haven't read a lot of leadership books that share personal narratives. But how can you talk about authenticity without real-life experiences? So I'll share another one with you.

My father died while I was writing this book and the last thing he asked me to do before he died was "Stand up for me." I've already expressed that my father and I had a very complex relationship. There were many things about him I didn't like. Reflecting back, he was a very sick man, but he always let my sister and me know how much he loved us. After being estranged for some time, on April 30, 2017, at 5:52 a.m., he sent me the following text message:

> Sweetheart, I only remember that I wanted y'all near me, and that's what I did. I thought, I was a fool; what I thought. My sincerest apology to you and your sister. I'm still adamant with my notwithstanding efforts! Pray for me real hard, as it's a father's desire to walk along every milestone. I'm so very proud of y'all's accomplishments. From me to you all with my only love, which is so deep that even I cannot fathom. Just stand up for your father, okay?

I don't think it was a coincidence that out of all the letters, cards, and messages my father sent me over the years, the one I received before we laid him to rest on June 11, 2017, asked me to stand up for him. Like many people in our society, although my father had never been diagnosed (to my knowledge) with a mental illness, he was emotionally unhealthy, to put it mildly. After all the things my father had done, he had the audacity to ask me to stand up for him.

And I did. Who would've known [certainly not me!] that I'd have positive memories to draw from to write a poem, which was a response to his last message, reassuring him that I would stand up for him?

Standing up for him was not about him—it was a reflection of who I am. I don't know the exact moment it happened, but I had found it in my heart to forgive him. Deep inside,

I knew that he was the best father that he could be. Similar to my mother, it wasn't until his death that I had a greater appreciation for him as my father. I couldn't change who he was. I couldn't erase his mistakes. But I could stand up for him by sharing more of the flattering things about him that a lot of people at his funeral probably never got to see.

Part of your role as a leader is to stand up for those you lead. There will come a time to show people who you truly are and what you're made of. You will know exactly what to say or do when that moment comes. One way this can be seen is how you respond when your team succeeds or fails. Your team will either build a tighter bond or it will gradually fall apart, simply based on your response. For example, when your team makes a mistake, do you disassociate and place blame? Or do you say, "It's not my fault, but it is my problem"?

Moment of Reflection

Think about a time when a leader took full credit for your idea, report, or project. Or maybe you made a mistake and your leader threw you under the bus. How did it feel? While that emotion is raw, would you want someone else to feel how you're feeling?

Don't check out yet—maybe that person was you. Have you ever taken credit for someone else's idea? Ever had the opportunity to stand up for someone but were frozen by fear? Let me be more specific: Have you ever had the opportunity to diffuse a rumor or stand up for someone's character, but you chose not to?

During one of my coaching sessions that seemed more like a therapy session, a leader we'll call Jon opened up about his relationship with a male colleague that he considered a friend we'll call Stephon. With intense despair in Jon's voice, he stated that the two of them always took breaks and lunch together, but recently, Stephon never seemed to be available. Yet Jon would see Stephon having lunch with other people in their department. Eventually, Jon worked up the courage to ask Stephon if he had done something wrong, and it all poured out: Stephon had distanced himself because their leader had told him that someone had told her that Jon was trying to sabotage him to get his position.

Let's pause for a moment so you can ponder what's wrong with this story. First, if Stephon was truly Jon's friend, he should've given his friend the benefit of the doubt. In the spirit of authenticity, Stephon could've confronted Jon with what was said to give him the opportunity to confirm or deny the accusation. Second, and more importantly, when the rumor was brought to the leader, she should've been a part of the solution, not the problem.

As a leader, if someone comes to you with "he said, she said," it's your responsibility to further investigate and coach all parties involved, starting with the person who brought you the rumor. Furthermore, until you've uncovered the facts and heard from all parties involved, an authentic leader should stand up for the accused because they are innocent until proven guilty. And even if the facts reveal that they are guilty, it's still a coaching opportunity. The last thing you want to do is get in the middle of the rumor like this leader did. Not only does it cause division, but it breaks trust within the team.

Research has shown that people don't quit their job—they quit their boss. This was true for me a few times in my career. Once, there was a position coming open for a production lead. Given my position at the time, this would've been a natural progression for me. As such, I interviewed for the position and was selected for the role. Oddly enough, I was told that I wouldn't be getting a pay increase, although it was a promotion, because "they" wanted to see if I was a good fit for the role. My leader told me that they'd re-evaluate my pay based on my performance in six months. I knew this wasn't right, but my boss presented it as though it was a good opportunity to take on a stretch assignment and get more exposure to position myself for leadership.

Six months passed. Twelve months passed, but still no talk of a pay increase. I got the production lead title when I started the position, but I should've received an increase as well. Not to mention, this new position came with a great deal of responsibility and added pressure from my peers, who didn't even want the position but didn't want to see me in it either. It was a stressful work environment that I quickly came to resent. I often wondered if my peers would've given me such a hard time if they had known that I never got a pay increase for a promotion that came with a new title and an overwhelming amount of work. Then, to add insult to injury, after I had been in the role for a little over a year, I requested a meeting with my boss to discuss my job performance and pay increase. And as soon as I brought up money, he immediately attacked my character, accusing me of only being in the role for the money.

Reflecting back, I wish I'd had a mentor or another leader who would've coached me to never take a promotion without a pay increase. Over my career, I have taken on a myriad of stretch assignments and I continue to volunteer, but this was different. Yes, I was seeking to learn a new skill set, but I was also looking to better myself by advancing my career. Before I was presented with this new opportunity, I trusted my leader and thought that he really cared about my well-being. But, given that he would have me take a promotion without pay and attack my character when I asked about compensation, it clearly revealed to me that he didn't care about me or the well-being of my family. I may never know if senior leadership asked him to approach me and the opportunity this way, but if they did, he should've stood up for me.

After being in the role for approximately eighteen months, I was consumed with resentment, specifically toward my boss. Although the work was stressful, I had it down to a science, so I probably would've hung in there if I'd felt like my leader had my back. Fortunately, one of the benefits of being in that new role, even without a pay increase, was that I got the opportunity to work with other departments that were more than interested to have me on their teams. As a result, I interviewed with two different departments and got offers from both. This put me in a position to choose the area that I thought would be a good fit for me and me for them.

You may be thinking that if he hadn't promoted me, I wouldn't have received exposure to the other two teams, and I won't argue with that. Even so, my new promotion was not a reflection of him but of my work ethic. In addition, I believe that what's for you is for you. When time and opportunity meet, nobody can stop, dictate, or control your success. Furthermore, yes, the compensation mattered, especially when I'd been consistently told in my twenty-three-year tenure that I was grossly underpaid when it was time for my yearly performance review. Nevertheless, his motives and lack of integrity caused me pain and resentment.

If you are a teacher, coach, boss, parent, or anyone in a position of authority, trust me, those you are leading are saying *"Please* stand up for me!" Here are some ways you can stand up for the people you lead:

- When someone accuses the person you're leading of a mistake or wrongdoing, invite them into a conversation, explaining the accusation and with sincerity. Let them know you want to hear their side of the story.

- If the accusation made against the person you're leading is true and the accused is present or included in the email communication, respond with "we" language, accepting shared responsibility; they're an extension of you. You can also acknowledge to the accuser that you'll be addressing the complaint without using accusatory language toward the employee in question.

- If someone you're leading is verbally attacked in your presence (including by email), speak up on the person's behalf so that they know that you have their back. You can also speak up for them if they're not present to set a precedent to others that you stand up for your people.

Pillar VII: Names

Going back to Biblical times, people were either given names or their names were changed to best represent their identity. For example, there was a character in the Bible named Jacob who was known as a trickster. As the story goes, he held on to his twin brother's heel when he was coming out of their mother's womb. Then he continued to live up to this name, even when he was older, as he tricked his father into believing that he was his older brother to steal his birthright. If you're not familiar with this story, later in life, Jacob's name was changed to Israel because God said he had wrestled with God and prevailed. In short, he was able to overcome his name: "the trickster."

In the twenty-first century, the meaning of names is just as popular. Parents search through books for baby names, looking for a positive meaning, while others choose the name of a significant family member. Some people give their babies names that they think are pretty or they like how they sound. No matter the reason, everyone's name has meaning. Only you can choose if you'll live up to it or not.

The Names pillar is of great importance to leading out of authenticity because, as previously stated, names matter—using someone's name makes them feel seen. Ever ask yourself, "Who in the hell am I?" My birth certificate says "Alvinnia Rochelle," my mom nicknamed me "Lady," my grandma called me "Cookie," friends at school referred to me by my government name, "Alvinnia," and I choose to go by Rochelle. Alvinnia is confident, direct, and handles business. Cookie is bashful and likes to hide. Lady has a hard exterior for protection while longing to be loved and accepted. And Rochelle is still becoming. I told you I'm simply complex. Even if I decided to only go by one name, it wouldn't matter, because my personality still has that range. All my personas have a purpose and are needed. Just like Dr. Jekyll and Mr. Hyde, Lady's self-doubt shows up at times that Alvinnia's confidence needs to rise up.

How simple would it be to only have to respond to one name? I wouldn't know. What I do know is that if I tried to overlook, dismiss, forget, or disregard any one of my names, I would lose part of my identity. One person, four names, one identity. Simply complex, right?

Now that you've become better acquainted with one of my personas, Lady, I would like to introduce you to Alvinnia (pronounced "Al-vin-yuh"). When I was in undergrad, I had a professor correct how I pronounced my name. He said based on how it's spelled, it "should" be pronounced "Al-vin-ne-yuh." His unsolicited pronunciation was arguably rude. Nonetheless, it kind of made sense, and given I couldn't recall how my mom or dad pronounced it, I'll answer to either pronunciation. Wondering how I got that name? Glad you asked. If you've been keeping up with my story, you know that my dad's name was Alvin, and Alvinnia simply derives from Alvin. I'm actually quite impressed whenever someone attempts to pronounce Alvinnia, and it puts a smile on my face when they pronounce it "correctly."

What is it like in the day and life of Alvinnia? First, it's a name that even in my forties I haven't gotten used to. When I was younger, other than students and teachers at school, no one called me Alvinnia. Interestingly enough, as far back as I can remember, nobody in my family or friend groups ever called me Alvinnia. Not unless it was used out of spite or a poor attempt to be humorous. When I did hear it, I was far removed from it. So much so, even when I reflect, I have no emotion to draw from, like Lady. Talk about a persona. "The person" called by that name was only going through the motions, only responding so as not to be rude. I had no connection to the name, which meant I probably didn't have a connection with the people who used it. It was a way to address me; a way to distinguish me from the other twenty-eight to thirty students in class.

By now, I'm sure you're thinking that I hate that name, but actually, I don't. I just can't relate to it. As you may recall, a lot of my childhood is spotty, especially elementary school. There're only a few memories that stand out to me. One was an example I shared earlier when I forged my grandmother's signature on my report card. Remember how I got busted? That's right! I spelled Margaret incorrectly. What can I say? Umm... I was never the spelling bee champion. You can probably imagine what happened next. Grandma came to the school without hesitation and beat my butt in front of my teacher. No charges were pressed, of course. Back then, lines were too blurred to distinguish between a much-needed spanking and child abuse.

Hey, female readers, did you know that guys still rank us based on looks? Yes, a male colleague wanted to share my "Who's a Hot Female" rank with me some years ago at work. But to prove that I wasn't that shallow, I abruptly declined. For some reason, he desperately wanted to share, but I refused to subject my self-esteem to what I knew to be a childhood game. To that end, my first exposure to this was in the fifth grade. I'll never forget seeing the list of the "prettiest" fifth-grade girls, and I was ranked number two. That was a surprise, even to me. Given that I was such a tomboy (or what some would today refer to as androgynous), I never would've expected to be a runner-up, at least not in looks.

So, who *is* Alvinnia? She's my foundation! The source of my identity. The name I use to be taken seriously when handling business. Alvinnia is used to be recognized by a former classmate, at a doctor's visit, placing a credit card reservation, or to pay a bill. I may choose to go by Rochelle, will even answer to Cookie or Lady, but my name is one of the few things my parents could give me, and I would never disown it or give it away.

Sorry, readers! I don't have a lot to say about where Cookie derives from, other than my grandma must've thought I was incredibly sweet. Growing up, my grandma wasn't the only person who referred to me as Cookie. It was common to hear Cookie or Lady while I was running around the neighborhood. The best theory I could come up with is that if the person in the neighborhood knew not just me but also my grandmother more personally, they called me Cookie because she did. However, if it was one of my friends' parents, they would call me Lady because their child called me Lady. What matters is that all these names matter to me and are a part of my identity.

Moment of Reflection

Once I heard someone say, "It's not what they call you—it's what you answer to." More importantly, what do you call yourself?

Does your given name or nickname accurately describe you? Is it a name you're proud to answer to? Do you have a connection with your name? Some therapists have their clients do an exercise called the Wheel of Fear. Given everything that I've shared (and a lot I haven't), yes, I've been to see a therapist once or twice. Around the same time my mother died, we were also dealing with some serious issues with our son. During a routine exam with my gynecologist of many years, he simply asked how I was doing. After giving me fatherly advice for over an hour (unheard of at a doctor's office, full of impatient patients, and for that, I'll be forever grateful), he strongly encouraged me to seek counseling.

Following trusted guidance, I scheduled my first therapy session. This was when my therapist pulled out this Wheel of Fear. Imagine the *Wheel of Fortune* spinner on the popular game show. This wheel had the same shape, but instead of prize amounts, it had fears. After having me look over all the fears, the therapist asked, "If the people closest to you thought (blank) about you, how would it make you feel?"

Why do you think she asked that? Think about the term "Wheel of Fear." Think about the people closest to you or people you admire and respect. Would you not say that their opinion of you holds a certain amount of weight? Maybe so much weight that if it got back to you that they called you (fill in your deepest fear), it could affect how you see yourself, even your confidence. But what's scarier is what you call yourself.

One of my favorite go-to books for self-improvement is *The Four Agreements* by Don Miguel Ruiz. In this small, easy-to-read, practical book, he makes a profound statement that I'm reminded of daily. In my own words, nobody can make you feel some way that you don't already feel about yourself. You shouldn't take it personally if someone calls you stupid, not unless you believe you're stupid. Even if someone calls you fat and you are overweight, you only give it power if you think that being overweight is negative. What I'm building up to is that our deepest fear shouldn't be what others call us, not even what we answer to (although it matters). What keeps us up at night is what we call ourselves.

Yes, names have meaning and words have power. Therefore, no matter what others say about you—good or bad—you have to see value in yourself. I was always told that you're never as good as people say you are or as bad as they say you are. Nobody should have the power to build you up or tear you down. Affirmation has to come from within. Knowing your self-worth is important because what you call yourself will influence how others see you and treat you.

As a leader, if you don't know your self-worth, chances are you struggle with encouraging and supporting the people you lead. Ironically, some of the most successful people are some of the most insecure people. This can be seen based on how they treat subordinates or people who can't do anything for them. Have you ever been in the position of the one being led and been frequently torn down or never affirmed by the one leading you? This is a red flag that your leader may have some unresolved identity issues that may negatively affect you.

When you're experiencing mistreatment, it can be confusing because, predicated on their position or title, you don't see yourself as a threat. As such, you're perplexed, trying to figure out why your coach, teacher, director, even parent seems to be jealous of you or verbally try to tear you down. No matter how hard you work or how much you contribute, they refuse to give you a compliment. Even worse, out of fear, they will devalue you. They're scared that if you know your worth or believe in yourself, you might leave them. Really? Yes, it's true.

Maybe you or someone you know have experienced this type of treatment in a platonic or romantic relationship. This person spends a lot of time creating a persona that is impressive to you and others, but deep inside, they have a negative depiction of themselves. As a result, they may think that you're a confident, hardworking, intelligent person, but they will never tell you. Consciously or unconsciously, holding back positive reinforcement or acknowledgment can be as damaging as calling you something offensive or demeaning. Sometimes, what's not said is more powerful than what is said, which is why I'm stressing the importance of knowing your self-worth.

You have to teach people how to treat you and what you're going to answer to. Having standards and knowing your worth does not make you arrogant or overly confident. It makes you a human worthy of dignity, fair treatment, and respect. If you're going to lead out of authenticity, you have to be honest with others and true to yourself. Playing yourself small or hiding in someone else's shadow is not a good example of a strong leader. Neither is tearing down someone to make yourself look good.

But before you can lead out of authenticity, you have to know yourself. So, what should I call you? Finish the sentence stem or incomplete sentence:

1. I'm at my best when I:

   _____

2. When I feel good about myself, I:

   _____

3. One of my strengths as a leader is:

   _____

4. When I make a mistake or poor decision, I:

   _____

5.   When my leader doesn't recognize my accomplishments, I:

_____

6.   I see the best in others when they:

_____

7.   When I want others to feel good about themselves, I:

_____

8.   When I see strengths in those I lead, I:

_____

9.   When someone I lead feels bad about a mistake or poor decision, I:

_____

10.   When someone I lead accomplishes a goal, I:

_____

Remember: what you think of yourself is often projected onto others. Therefore, the purpose of this exercise is to identify patterns or inconsistencies in how you treat yourself compared to how you treat other people.

Leader note: The example I didn't share is the person who may have a bad self-perception. You know who you are. Although you're self-critical and hard on yourself, you feel better about yourself when you build up others. Do you think this makes you better than the leader who can't affirm others? Certainly not. This too is unhealthy. To lead out of authenticity, it's important not only to lift others up but also to be just as kind to yourself. Otherwise, you'll self-sabotage, or even worse, give up your position, thinking others would be a better fit. I don't want that for you; more significantly, you don't want that for yourself.

You have a purpose. Not because I said so, but because there is only one of you. That means that you were created with something specific that the world needs. If you don't see it and believe it, the rest of us are missing out. In the opening of this chapter, I shared a lot of names that I was given and how they each have shaped my identity. But what's crucial is not what you call me, not what I answer to, but what I know to be true about myself.

What's true about you? That's what I'm going to call you.

Pillar VIII: Self-Love

*"For I know the plans I have for you," declares
the Lord, "plans to prosper you and not harm
you, plans to give you hope and a future."*
—Jeremiah 29:11 NIV

There are many types of love and not all can be defined. Many still ask the question: what is love? According to Aristotle and Plato, there are several types of love, but I'll only focus on a few. The most commonly known and used love is *agape*. Agape love is unconditional, the type of love that we can even have for strangers, not expecting it in return. Another type of love is *eros*. Unlike agape, eros love is more romantic, the type of passionate love that we have for a romantic partner. Then there's *philia*. This is a friendly type of love that is founded on goodwill to another, associated with mutual benefits.

The love that we're going to focus on is *philautia*. Ah... the love of self. Self-love can be healthy or unhealthy. In ancient Greece, a person who placed himself above the gods could be accused of hubris, which was frowned upon. A more commonly used word today would be a narcissist, someone with an inflated ego who is in love with themselves. If you're in a relationship with someone like that, I've read many blogs that say you should run. The self-love I encourage you to focus on, however, is akin to self-esteem and self-confidence.

Why is self-love vital for someone to lead out of authenticity? When someone has a healthy love for themselves, they are able to genuinely invest in others without fear of rejection. This pillar is so critical because it allows the leader to lead from a place of growth, understanding, acceptance, forgiveness, and trust.

"I might as well be me. Everyone else is taken," says Oscar Wilde. Accepting me for me wasn't easy because I didn't like me—for years. I struggled with self-love. I didn't have self-worth. I didn't see anything good in me or about me. I believed that everybody was born with a purpose except me. Having that mindset was contrary to the silent whisper constantly telling me that I was born for greatness. Every time I would accomplish something, I would hear "Greater" in my soul, basically saying there was more work that needed to be done. Until this day, I still struggle with this dichotomy. It didn't matter what other people thought of me because I didn't project the strong woman who struggled with self-worth and won!

The thing about projections is that people will treat you based on how you carry yourself and the energy you give off. Therefore, if you exude confidence, assurance, and high self-esteem, people will treat you with dignity and respect. But if they sense weakness, low self-esteem, or defeat, they will look for ways to control or manipulate you. Trust me, I've experienced both.

Honestly, out of all my personas, I struggle with Lady the most. She may be a part of my identity, but often, I try to separate from her because she represents a huge part of the mistakes I've made and the pain I've experienced in life. It's not that Lady won't die—she can't die! She exudes more strength, confidence, boldness, and courage than I give her credit for. The once-guarded, rebellious, and aloof teenager/young adult, whom nobody would take advantage of, mistreat, abandon, or reject again, blossomed into a vulnerable woman who can give and receive love.

It doesn't matter if you call me Alvinnia, Rochelle, Lady, or Cookie, because I'll answer to all of them. It doesn't matter if one struggles with self-love, low self-esteem, or personal identity. It doesn't matter if you prefer one name or persona over another. What matters is that God took every layer and every broken piece of me and mended it all together into a masterpiece as simple yet as complex as a creation could be.

When he said, "Come forth and take your place in the world," I responded, "Who, me?"

And God asked, "Why not you?"

Let's be clear. I unapologetically believe in Jesus, but I realize and respect that you may believe in something or someone else, possibly nothing at all. So, while that voice telling me to find my place in the world is God, what is that voice for you? You are worthy of love, and self-love will determine how well you love others.

Moment of Reflection

If you are leading in any capacity, it could be that you're a natural-born leader, you applied for the position, or you were put in the position, but what's paramount is that you show up. Not all leaders are born; many are made, even if you didn't ask for it. Do I believe everyone has a purpose? Yes! Do I believe everyone is meant to lead? No!

In training classes, coaching sessions, and leadership courses that I've conducted over the years, this question always comes up: "Do you believe leaders are made or born?" Both. In part because I look at the word "leader" as a verb, not a noun. I believe that there are people who were born with intrinsic leadership traits and characteristics that make leading look effortless. However, others may not possess what some experts or thought leaders would define as leadership skills, but these attributes can be learned. Before sharing an example of how leaders can be made who may not have been born with innate leadership characteristics, let's explore some of the most commonly used words or characteristics used to describe a leader:

- Communication
- Dependability
- Empathy
- Positivity
- Motivation
- Self-awareness
- Creativity
- Accountability

You can add or take away from this list. More essentially, use it as a point of reference.

The example I'm going to walk you through will be based on a call center experience. To that end, I encourage you to use your imagination to connect this example to your field. The purpose is to show you that leaders can be made, even if they're not born with natural leadership skills.

Imagine a person was just hired at Company A as a claims specialist—let's call her Keisha. Keisha's main job function is adjudicating claims correctly once they've been electronically submitted into a system. Their department goal is to process seventeen claims per hour (CPH) with a 98 percent accuracy rate. If these goals are consistently met throughout the year, when it's time for Keisha's annual review, she would be considered a Full Contributor, which is a good review.

But wait a minute. Before signing off on a good annual review, you have to factor in more than just her metrics; you also have to consider how Keisha shows up. This includes but is not limited to behavior, attendance, attitude, etc. If all these are met, she would be considered Demonstrating, which is even higher than being a Full Contributor, because she's meeting her metrics, competencies, and contributions with a positive attitude.

For the last three years, Keisha, who was hired as a claims specialist, has exceeded all her metrics, competencies, and contributions. She has been processing nineteen CPH with a 100 percent accuracy rate, she has perfect attendance, and she doesn't have any behavior issues.

Now there's an opening for a supervisor position and Keisha is strongly encouraged to apply. With slight reluctance, not sure if she's ready for a leadership position, she applies, gets the job, and embarks on her journey in the call center as a leader.

Early in her new position as supervisor, she hasn't fully tapped into the leadership skills or traits that are going to make her an effective leader. As a matter of fact, she wasn't necessarily promoted for leadership characteristics anyway. What made Keisha an attractive candidate was her high job performance, perfect attendance, and positive attitude. Therefore, it only made sense that her natural/innate skills of dependability, accountability, and motivation transferred into her new role. The more Keisha got acclimated into her role, the more her manager started to notice that she lacked the leadership skills needed to build a high-performing team.

With that in mind, when she started getting feedback on job performance during their monthly one-on-one, there was a recurring theme that she needed to improve her communication and empathy skills with her employees.

Does this come as a surprise to you? If so, it shouldn't. It is very common in operational departments such as call centers, sports teams, factory work, or any profession where people are primarily promoted because of their performance (how good they are with systems and processes) rather than observable leadership skills (how good they are with people; if they are approachable, whether they care).

The good news is that leaders can be made! With additional soft-skills training, coaching, and leadership development, I believe that you can make these high performers into effective leaders. If your organization doesn't have internal training, coaching, and development opportunities, you could reach out to a consultancy firm or an individual consultant like myself to meet your development needs.

Here's a coaching scenario that I've used with clients with similar needs for leader development. Given that this individual is new to a leadership role, we're going to go through six weekly one-hour sessions together. In session one, I'll do an intake to identify areas of opportunity given to me by the coachee. At this point in the coaching sessions, as the coach and consultant, I have been given feedback on this leader, their metrics, strengths, opportunities, and anything else from their leader that can serve as a guide in these sessions. But more significantly, as a coach, I want to approach this relationship as unbiased as possible. Starting with an intake gives them an opportunity to get out their concerns, frustrations, current state, and expected outcomes.

In the second session, I'll do an evaluation and put together a personalized model for their coaching sessions. Then, each week, they'll be given homework to put into practice: tips, tools, and resources shared during our sessions. This also gives them an opportunity to share with me what worked, what didn't work, or if additional guidance is needed.

By week six, it's time to acknowledge and celebrate all their progress and successes. At this point, they will be given a continuous improvement plan so that they can track their progress and opportunities for improvement after our coaching sessions. In addition, I'll periodically send them up-to-date, industry-related resources, articles, and leadership tips for continuous growth and improvement. More importantly, by the end of our six weeks together, I'm confident that they will be well-equipped to lead with their head and heart.

It's okay if a high-performing individual doesn't possess all the characteristics some believe makes a good leader. What matters is that they are coachable, willing to learn, and open to growing. What should also be noted is that it will take more effort and energy for leaders who don't innately have leadership characteristics, but they should be confident that with guidance from a supportive leader, they will make continuous progress in these areas.

I've just shared how a leader who is a high producer but doesn't possess strong leadership characteristics can be developed into a successful leader. It will take some self-love. Self-love helps you to see the potential others see in you. If this example reminds you of you, and you're thinking, "Who? Me? A leader?" quickly shift your thinking to, "Why not me?"

Pillar IX: Self-Acceptance

An identity would seem to be arrived
at by the way in which the person
faces and uses his experience.
—James Baldwin

The dictionary defines acceptance as "the action or process of being received as adequate or suitable, typically to be admitted into a group." But the type of acceptance this pillar is focusing on is acceptance of self. Acceptance of where we come from. Acceptance of the people, places, and things that have helped shape us. It is impossible to lead out of authenticity without acceptance of who we are and the experiences that made us. Resisting the truth doesn't make it go away or make it any less real. It only keeps us in a state of misery as we try to drink it away, work it away, shop it away, eat it away, or whatever addiction you may use to avoid accepting the truth—your truth. This pillar is going to challenge you to accept all of you: the choices you've made that you can't change, your physical appearance, your personality, and the truth about what makes you, *you*.

If you've lived long enough, I'm sure you've been told who, what, or how you should be. Maybe you can relate to one or two of these: You should wear your hair straight. You should let your hair grow out. With that receding hairline, you should go bald. You should be more like your brother. You should be more like your sister. You should go back to school. You should lose weight. You should pick up a few pounds. You should join the fitness center. Right about now, you're probably thinking, "People should mind their own business! Who I am works for me!"

I don't know about you, but I've spent too many years trying to be what other people thought I should be.

After years of rediscovering myself
over and over again, I learned one vital
thing: *if I listened to what everyone said
I should be or should do, I'd be insane.*

Everybody has an opinion on what's best for you. Given that everyone's feedback on what you should do or how you should be fluctuates based on their personal preferences, can you imagine the emotional roller coaster that would be racing through your mind if you took it all into consideration? Guess what? To be accepted and fit in, I tried, but you don't have to.

If you choose to learn from others' experiences, you'll save wasted time and energy. When I was younger, in my late teens, I had what some would refer to as a shapely figure. Not being fully secure in myself, I tried to change how I walked because girls who were insecure about their figure would tease me, especially how I walked. They would say things like, "Look at her, she thinks she's cute," or "She thinks she's better than us, but look at how she walks."

These comments were always followed by laughter or threats. Generally, when people say things like, "You think you're smart," "cute," or "better," it's what they think about you, and they probably have low self-esteem. But rather than build you up with a compliment, they choose to tear you down with insults. Sadly, as an adult, I still get this same negative energy from a lot of women in the forms of passive-aggressive behavior, jabs, or manipulation. This form of harassment created a complex in me.

Keep in mind that when I was younger, I wanted to hide and didn't want to draw attention to myself. Even more, I wanted to be liked. I wanted to fit in. Yet, other than wearing baggy clothes, which wasn't my style at that time, I chose to change how I walked. Logically, it made sense to me. I broke it down like this: If I heard women making snarky remarks whenever I walked into the room or walked by a guy who would take a double-take at my behind, it only made sense to change the walk. It wasn't until an ex-boyfriend, who would always refer to me as "a queen," asked, "Why do you walk like that?" which challenged me to realize that I had changed my walk to not draw unwanted attention. Talk about a life-changing question. Here I'd thought I was being unassuming, but by the look in his eyes, he was saying, "Why are you walking like a duck?"

Like most people, it took me until I was older to appreciate how God chose to create me, figure and all. What's sad is that I know many of you can relate to trying to change something about you, not because you have a problem with it, but from others projecting their insecurities onto you. If you're anything like me, you struggle with your own insecurities, so you don't need anyone else adding to them.

Another part of my identity that is very unique is my speech. Call it a dialect, maybe it's diction, but whatever it is, my speech is not just based on the region where I grew up. There are certain words that I pronounce in a way that will either make you chuckle, pretend you didn't hear it, or feel the need to correct me. Most people choose the latter, not realizing that if I could pronounce it differently, I would. I was in speech classes throughout elementary school and should probably still be in them today. But I've learned to embrace it as one of the things that makes me unique. Actually, my voice is often recognized before I'm seen, because I'm told and would agree that I have a distinctive voice. This is not to say that I've never tried to work on my dialect or pronouncing words to sound more English instead of "Rochellisms," but I've made it work for me.

The point I'm trying to make is that you were created to be just as you are. Therefore, if you have a Southern drawl, big butt, pointy ears, naturally curly hair, deep voice, or chicken legs, those are all things (without too much effort or surgery) that you cannot change. But what you can change is to stop allowing other people's opinions of you to negatively influence how you see yourself.

So the next time someone says, "You should be . . ." you say, "Who I am may not work for you, but it works for me."

Moment of Reflection

Let's get to the heart of *leading out of authenticity*. This chapter is about you being true to yourself and accepting the things that make you, you. Take a moment to rate the following things about yourself on a scale of 0–10, with 10 representing something you absolutely love and 0 being something you strongly dislike.

1. Personality _____

2. Weight _____

3. Memory _____

4. Looks _____

5. Intellect _____

6. Race _____

7. Gender _____

8. Empathy _____

9. Generosity _____

10. Voice _____

Now I want you to be more specific:

1. Shape of your nose _____

2. Size of your feet _____

3. How you receive feedback _____

4. How you give feedback _____

5. Patience _____

6. Assertiveness _____

7. How you're shaped _____

8.   How you speak _____

9.   Size of your stomach _____

10.   Shade of your skin _____

Let's see if who you are works for you. The highest score is 200. Scores from 0 to 67, you probably have a low self-image. Scores from 68 to 133, you probably think moderately well of yourself. And scores from 134 to 200, you probably have a healthy view of self.[5]

We all have things about ourselves we don't like or wish we could improve. Some things we can work on without drastic or stressful measures, such as our personality, patience, demeanor, appearance, or weight. Yet there are other things that we simply can't change, such as race, gender, or body shape, without potential life-threatening consequences. There's a lot of people who don't have low metabolism or other health factors fighting against them who could lose weight with a healthy diet and exercise. But even once they lose the weight, it doesn't mean that they'll be content with their size or shape. For example, being someone whose weight has always fluctuated up and down by ten to twenty pounds, I've never been able to control where I lost the weight.

Have you ever tried to change your personality? How long did it last? Let's say you're easily frustrated, impatient, or reactive. According to Daniel Goleman, an emotional intelligence guru, if you have high self-awareness, you could improve these behaviors. But it's important to note that before you can improve any behavior, you first have to be aware of it. In the book *Emotional Intelligence 2.0* by Travis Bradberry and Jean Greaves, only 36 percent of the people they tested were able to accurately identify their emotions as they happened.[6] So, for argument's sake, let's say you have low self-awareness. Does this mean you can't change? No. But it's going to take a lot of intentionality and energy to improve perceived negative behaviors that are natural for you.

Still on the topic of personality, let's say you'd like to be more thoughtful and generous. These are perceived positive qualities, right? Again, these are things you can work on, maybe with an accountability partner or calendar reminders of what to give, who to give it to, and when to give it to them.

But if this is not how you're inherently wired, to be consistent, you're going to have to raise your level of consciousness and awareness. This is no excuse not to try, but it may be more beneficial for everybody if you focus on your strengths and the things that come naturally to you. Everyone was created with different gifts, talents, personalities, sizes, shapes, and features to make this world a beautiful place. It would make everyone more comfortable if we could just absorb the parts of people that make us feel good, but we have to learn how to take a person's good with their bad. (And just to be clear, this excludes any form of emotional or verbal abuse. I would never encourage anyone to adapt to that.) With intentionality, I kicked this chapter off with how you view yourself before moving to how others view you.

Now we're going to go a little deeper and possibly open some wounds: What things have been said to you to tear you down? And what has been said to you that has given you a complex?

Growing up, when us kids would tease each other, a common response was "Sticks and stones may break my bones, but names will never hurt me." As much as I wish those words had a magical power to make hurtful words dissipate, you and I both know it isn't true. Abuse of any kind is unhealthy and shouldn't be tolerated.

One of the things I remember as a child is being given the choice of a punishment (typically, taking privileges away) or a spanking. More times than not, I chose the latter. Why? The spanking only stung for a few moments, but the punishment typically lasted for a couple of weeks. Not to mention, before my grandmother would spank me, she would always say, "This is going to hurt me more than it's going to hurt you," or the absolute worst: "I'm not mad. I'm disappointed." As a child, hearing that didn't make me feel any better. But when I became a parent, it hurt me when I took my children's privileges away, spoke to them harshly, or used any other form of discipline.

As adults, unlike the courtesy my grandmother extended to me, we're not given the option of how to receive a punishment. More often than not, when we make a mistake, frustrate someone, or someone wants to control us, they use the silent treatment or verbally attack us. One method is no better than the other. They both are unhealthy and leave a lasting, damaging impact. At one time or another, most people have been on the giving or receiving end of such punishments. Many psychologists believe that this behavior is carried over to adulthood from childhood, which will carry over to how we lead, if we don't recognize and get help for it.

In the book *The Four Agreements* by Don Miguel Ruiz, he talks about how people will project their insecurities onto you, and when you receive it, it's like you're taking poison. They may or may not believe what they're saying to you. The point is, it's not their place to build you up or tear you down. Ruiz goes on to say that even when someone says he's amazing, he accepts the compliment, but he doesn't hold on to it, because he knows he's amazing even if no one tells him. In other words, if no one ever says he's amazing, does it mean he's not? Or if someone says he's stupid, does it mean he is? No. Never give another person the power to build you up or tear you down. Your value and self-worth have to come from within.

You have to know who you are and be okay with who you are despite what other people say about you. Woefully, thanks to cortisol, which assists with memory formulation, we tend to hold on to the negative things that people say about us longer than the positive things. For example, out of one hundred, you could receive ninety-eight extraordinary survey results, but your brain would hold on to the negative two. This is why self-acceptance has to be paramount. You have to be good with who you are.

Ways to Make Sure *You* Work for You

1. **Build a relationship with yourself.** Spend time getting to know you. Instead of spending so much time trying to accommodate what

you think everyone else wants you to be, why not spend that time and energy discovering and embracing who you are? When you do, you give others permission to do the same. How can you expect anyone else to accept who you are if you don't?

2.   **Be honest with yourself.** We all have flaws and things about ourselves we don't like. There's nothing worse than lying to yourself. You don't have to share this with anybody else. But I'm encouraging you to unmask, be vulnerable, and be true to yourself. Since we're on this self-discovery journey together, I'm going to take a risk and share with you that I have big feet. To my knowledge, there's no surgery I can have to change it. Buying smaller shoes for the appearance of smaller feet will only torture me, so a long time ago, I accepted that I have big feet and I need to be okay with it. Sure, when I see people with small feet like my daughter Jessie, whose feet look cute in any type of shoes, a little envy rises up, but before that thought turns into a negative behavior, I give her a compliment and focus on how my feet serve me well. And it helps to keep up with my pedicures.

3.   **Discern who you can be vulnerable with.** You have to be selective about who you trust with your heart and insecurities. If not, when others

who haven't put in the work like you start to feel insecure or jealous of your newfound freedom, they'll exploit your insecurities and use them against you. Therefore, to protect yourself, only pull back those layers when a healthy relationship has been built on trust, truth, and integrity. Err on the side of caution until it's safe to go there. The importance of being honest with yourself is that nine times out of ten, if you see something as a flaw, others probably do too. Remember, everyone isn't as kind as you are, so if someone wants to hurt you, they'll use that flaw against you unless you've already exposed it. Instantly, their attack loses its power. If it's something you can change and choose to, go for it! If it's something you can't change, can't afford to change, or are too scared to change, accept it. Shortly, there will be ways to identify unhealthy relationships in this chapter.

4. **Find things about yourself that you like.** To like yourself or anything about you does not make you a narcissist. As a matter of fact, the more you're secure in who you are, the kinder you are to others. There's something about yourself that you really like (hopefully, a few things), but in the interest of fake humility, you play yourself down so that the "confidence moderators" won't feel the need to keep you humble.

Guess what? They're going to try to control how you should view yourself anyway, so why not keep your power? Appreciate your legs, skin tone, personality, hair, or intellect. Enjoy being *you*!

5.   **Be as kind to yourself as you are to others.** Yes, there are mean girls and bad boys who get pleasure in tearing down others, but that's not you. You're the person who likes to put a smile on someone's face with a kind gesture, word of encouragement, gift, or surprise. Even when you're at your lowest, you find enough strength to build others up. Are you as kind to yourself? If not, start now.

If we're going to build a relationship, I have to be honest with you. The truth is, I haven't mastered this. Like many of you, I am my own worst critic. I don't need anybody else to tear me down—I can do that all by myself. This is probably why I attract people who feed off my energy to feel better about themselves. If this is you, do not just glance over this section.

Bonus tip: If someone is *not* secure in who they are—their looks, their job, their intellect, their family, their home, their car, or their life—they will try to tear you down. Surprisingly, they may not even be aware that they're doing it.

Signs of Emotionally Unhealthy Relationships

- The person wants to control your confidence and self-esteem. When you're around them, you feel the need to play yourself down. They are masters at tearing you down to build you back up. This makes them feel good about themselves, and more importantly to them, it keeps you in your place. They'll make sure you never think too highly of yourself.

- You can't be honest with the person about your aspirations, successes, or accomplishments without them minimizing your experiences.

- They are toppers. If you share good news, theirs is better, or if you have bad news, theirs is worse.

- They play mind games. They pretend they are talking about someone else's situation, poor behavior, or flaws, but you have a strong sense they are really talking about you. Trust your gut—they are.

- They'll hold back compliments or well-wishes on special occasions such as your birthday. Again, they don't want you to feel too special. Note: if they do give you a compliment, don't be surprised if it's followed with a jab, typically when you express genuine gratitude. However, if you play it down, you might be safe for a little while.

• One day, you'll get the courage to tell them how much they've hurt you and how they've made you feel, and they'll put it back on you. They'll tell you how sensitive you are and "if" they've hurt or offended you, then they're sorry. They're probably an emotional manipulator.

Signs of Emotionally Healthy Relationships:

• They want to hear all about the good things that are going on in your life and are genuinely happy for you.

• Their actions match their words. Not only will they tell you how they feel about you, but they will also show you through their actions. If you are in a play, singing in a concert, coaching a Little League team, speaking at an event, have an art show, or are doing something you're passionate about, they want to be there. This does not mean that they will make it to everything, but they'll definitely want to show up for you in more than just words.

- They make time for you. Everyone is busy in our Western culture, especially if the person is ambitious and driven, but they want you to know that you matter to them, so they'll make time to talk to you, take a walk with you, or go for coffee or tea or maybe a meal. During your time together, they're not multitasking, texting, or looking at social media.

- They want you to feel special. They have no problem encouraging you and celebrating your successes. I have to give a special shout-out to my friend Cori. There is not one time in our friendship that I've ever sensed jealousy from her. Not once has she ever tried to tear me down. Anytime I share good news, aspirations, or new opportunities, she's always happy for me. I never feel the need to play myself down around her.

- They are easy to talk to about anything. There's a judgment-free zone with them. They make it safe to be honest and vulnerable with them. You don't have to worry about them sharing your secrets or using your words against you in later conversations as a chess move or to make you feel guilty.

Who I am works for me!
Please repeat after me:
Who I am works for me!

I had to spend a lot of time on this section, especially "Be as Kind to Yourself as You Are to Others," because if you are a leader who is or has been in an emotionally abusive relationship, there's a chance that you can be that person who is doing what has been done to you to others. From what I've been told by therapists, when someone has been in a physically or emotionally abusive relationship, they are either nothing like their abuser, which means they work hard to not inflict the pain they've endured on others. Or they become the abuser. Subconsciously or not, they treat people the way they were treated. Either way, they survived, and in a sick way they think they are fine, but hurt people tend to hurt people. As a leader, you have too much power and influence over those you lead. For every life we touch, positively or negatively, many other lives are affected.

If we want this world to be a better place, we have to do a better job of lifting people up instead of tearing them down. For those leaders who want to help create a world full of hope, peace, joy, and opportunities for all people, you have to lead out of authenticity, starting with *you* working for *you*! This may mean that you have to disconnect from those unhealthy relationships that keep you in a place of low self-esteem and low self-worth.

Pillar X: Self-Worth

We ask ourselves, "Who am I to be
brilliant, gorgeous, talented, fabulous?"
Actually, who are we not to be?
—Marianne Williamson

The pillar of self-worth is so essential because it influences your attitude and behavior. Self-worth has a significant impact on how you lead because, similar to self-love, self-worth is based on how you treat others. People with high self-worth are typically generous with compliments and often try to build others up. Unfortunately, people with low self-worth may try to make others feel bad about themselves to ensure they have company. The dictionary defines worth as "the value equivalent to that of someone or something under consideration; the level at which someone or something deserves to be valued or rated." If this is true, who determines the level at which someone "deserves" to be valued or rated? The obvious answer is *you* do. You not only determine someone's worth to you but you also determine your own self-worth—and you won't be able to lead authentically without it.

I'm 5 foot 5 inches and 165 pounds (give or take a few pounds, depending on the day or season). I have what my husband would describe as caramel-brown skin; dark-brown eyes; a pudgy nose; full lips; thin, arched eyebrows; long fingers; big feet; a small frame at the top; and rotund at the bottom. My personality is a mix between sanguine and choleric; I'm highly intuitive, harmonious, relational, honest, enthusiastic, and wear my feelings on my sleeve (sanguine). Yet I'm also self-motivated, focused, driven, organized, and an executor (choleric).

Most days, at home, at work, at the grocery store, or at social gatherings, I'm jovial, outgoing, friendly, and encouraging. I want everyone to feel accepted, appreciated, and loved. However, when in spaces with large groups or around people where I feel judged or unsafe, I tend to withdraw or can seem off-putting. In most formal or professional group settings, I won't be the first to speak up, but I will make a decision if nobody else can make one. I can take control, but I don't have to be in charge. I have a strong personality, and if you believe in zodiac signs, I'm an Aries and we're known to be natural-born leaders. When you mix that complexity with my passion and newly discovered assertiveness, it can feel overwhelming for some people, in a good or bad way.

Once, I was asked what animal I most identify with. My response was the eagle because it's the king of the sky, soaring high above everything and everybody. Yet I also identify with the lion, the king of the jungle. Maybe I am a natural-born leader, dominating the sky and the land, but I don't always feel like it. I often wonder: is that the person I aspire to be or have the potential to be? Because I don't always feel confident, assertive, or courageous. At best, most days I wake up positive, with a sense of purpose to conquer the world.

But there are still those days when I have to fight one of my biggest opponents: mediocrity. No disrespect to being ordinary. I believe we're all ordinary, but we have the opportunity to make a difference in extraordinary ways. I'm confident that I'm one of many ordinary people created to do extraordinary things, even if not on a large platform. On occasion, I ask myself, "Why can't you just be comfortable with what you've accomplished and where you're at in life?" My response to myself and those who either have lower expectations of me or think I've accomplished more than I recognize is "I can be content but not complacent. There's still too much work in the world to do."

Some of you may be able to relate to all or at least part of this. I believe it boils down to self-love and self-worth. It wasn't until I accepted Jesus as Lord and Savior that I felt worthy. Worthy of love, even worthy to live. Everyone— parents, romantic partners, children, and friends—has their own way of showing us we're worthy. Parents set our first example of what self-worth looks like. If you had affectionate parents who were huggers and used terms of endearment, you probably grew up feeling worthy of their affection, worthy of their love. Conversely, if you had parents who were cold, distant, and aloof, never outwardly expressing how they felt, this could have made you feel unworthy. But let's not dismiss that some of you may have had parents who were physically there but emotionally unavailable, or you had parents who were not present due to death or substance abuse. What all of this has in common is distance, which often feels like rejection or the lack of emotional support in any relationship and can either take away or contribute to one's self-worth.

What's wrong with even the healthiest example of love aforementioned is that you can't control it. You can't make someone love you or not love you. No matter how much we try, can we really teach someone how to love us? What's crucial is that we love ourselves; this is where true self-worth comes from. Way too often, we tend to define our worth based on external, superficial things such as looks, cars, houses, or how successful our children are. But we can't expect someone else to deem us worthy if we don't know it for ourselves. Sure, we all have things about our appearance, personality, and flaws about ourselves we don't like, but we have to trust that we were created with perfection in mind. As such, we are worthy just as we are.

It was imperative for me to open this chapter by describing myself, right down to the size of my feet and the shape of my hands, because it took a long time to truly feel worthy as I am. This happened when I accepted Christ and embraced the agape love he has for me. Coming from a disadvantaged, dysfunctional background with abandonment issues, I didn't always have a sense of self-worth. When I was able to accept that Jesus loves me—not despite me—because he created me in his image, I was able to start loving myself, including everything about me.

Self-worth has to come from within. No one can give it to you. If that's what you're waiting on, or you're getting a false sense of it and that's what you're depending on, you'll never feel good about yourself. Once you accept that there's only one of you, the only model of its kind, custom-made, an original never to be replicated, you'll never compare yourself with or be jealous of others, because you're exactly who you were created to be.

Moment of Reflection

The last few chapters were meant to build off each other because my goal is to build you up to lead out of authenticity. Self-love is when you recognize your flaws and imperfections but love yourself anyway. You no longer walk around on eggshells to keep so-called friends. You no longer need people to make you feel loved; you want friends to share life's precious moments with. An indicator that a person has a healthy love for themselves is when they're able to open their heart without fear of rejection. When you love yourself, everyone who crosses your path is a beneficiary of that love.

Self-acceptance is about accepting your identity—who you are, your DNA, and your mistakes. It focuses on the importance of being the person you were created to be, even if it means disconnecting or disassociating from people who are unhealthy for you. You believe in yourself, despite coming from a dysfunctional family or disadvantaged background or any mistakes you've made. Those things don't define you, so never allow anyone to play on your insecurities to mistreat you or try to control you. You accept the truth about who you are and where you come from as a source of strength and compassion for others.

Self-worth is no longer needing validation from others. This is not to say that you don't want to be recognized for a job well done or to be appreciated by loved ones. That makes you human. Having self-worth means you no longer seek out other people's approval. You can always tell if someone has self-worth based on how they treat others. You can open up and be vulnerable, knowing that complimenting someone else doesn't take anything away from you. You can even share knowledge or teach people what you do, knowing you're still needed because they can't do it like you.

In this chapter, I was very vulnerable with you, sharing my weight, shape, and other personal things about me. I did this intentionally because I want to be free to be authentically who I was created to be, and I want you to be free too. Just know that self-love, self-acceptance, and self-worth do come at a cost. If you haven't already made the decision to embrace yourself, let me help prepare you for some possible risks. It's true: for every action, there's a reaction. But there's always the power and beauty of living your truth, which comes with benefits that I'll share too.

The Risks of Choosing Self-Love, Self-Acceptance, and Self-Worth

When you choose to love and embrace all of you, despite society's false narrative that this is pride and arrogance, it can be lonely. I wish we lived in a society where you could openly love yourself, accept yourself, and have self-worth, and people would be happy with your newfound freedom. But they won't until they've reached that level for themselves.

Disappointingly, as stated in the previous chapters, this powerful concept won't work for those who struggle with identity issues and low self-esteem. You will intimidate them. It doesn't matter how kind you are or how much you encourage others to love themselves. A lot of people are not comfortable with this level of self-embracement. This doesn't mean that they don't like you. Someone can like you but not understand you, or even be jealous of you. For this reason, they will stay clear of you. You'll probably gain a few distant admirers, but they dare not get too close to you. And the ones who dare to get to know you, if they're not secure in who they are, will become the emotional manipulators I described to you in the previous chapter.

The Benefits of Choosing Self-Love, Self-Acceptance, and Self-Worth

If you make the bold decision to love and embrace all of you, at the expense of not gaining or losing some disingenuous relationships, you'll give the people you lead hope that they can do the same.

Look at you! The role model of self-love, self-acceptance, and self-worth. You are free, you are healed, you are whole! Sure, you'll still make mistakes. To be human is to be flawed, but this newfound love for self will transform the lives of many. So much will flow out of you now that you're embracing all of you. You'll be that leader who builds people up, not tear them down. You'll be out there encouraging people to be their best selves. You'll mentor and coach others to do what you do or inspire them to do what they're passionate about. I'm encouraged at the thought of a world full of confident, creative, positive, fun, loving, and humble people who are inspiring others to do the same. I congratulate and applaud you for simply being you.

Reflections

Pillar XI: Authenticity

Ah . . . this is the pillar we all aspire to. Yes, even I.

What is authenticity? The Merriam-Webster dictionary defines authentic as "worthy of acceptance or belief as conforming to or based on fact; conforming to an original so as to reproduce essential features; not false; true to one's own personality, spirit, or character." If you are a leader of people—in your home, at work, at school, at church, on a board, or in the community—leading out of authenticity will help transform our world. A lot of companies are starting departments specifically dedicated to inclusion and diversity, which is a great thing. The goal is to ensure that everyone has a sense of belonging despite our differences. But the only way we're going to see the change that we hope for is when words like inclusion and diversity aren't just buzz words or used to positively reflect one's company, but they become a part of each individual's DNA and core values.

Being authentic is much easier said than done. But until we can accept our own true identity, character, personality, and everything else that is woven into our existence, we'll never accept others for who they are. That said, you don't need to be authentic to lead—you may even be a good leader—but to be a transformational leader, I encourage you to consider leaning into this pillar.

"Encourager," "teacher," and "servant leader" are three words I would use in an elevator speech to describe myself. Achiever, Learner, Input, Connectedness, and Intellection are my top five strengths according to the assessment in Tom Rath's book *StrengthsFinder 2.0*. Real Colors' assessment shows that I can identify with sanguine and choleric personalities. According to Myers and Briggs, depending on the day, my results have shown that I can be an INFJ (introverted, intuitive, feeling, and judging), but most consistently, it shows that I'm an ENFJ (extroverted, intuitive, feeling, and judging)—someone who not only likes to help others but also actually enjoys bringing out the best in others. The final assessment result I'll share is the Enneagram that says that I'm a type 2 (The Helper) and type 5 (The Thinker). Given that I've taken each of those assessments (some more than twice), they paint an accurate picture of who I believe I am. But the question still remains: is Rochelle my persona (how I want people to perceive me) or my true self (the person I was created to be)?

Cookie, Lady, and Alvinnia all make up the person that is today known as Rochelle. Based on my DNA, environment, and life experiences, I would like to think that I've finally embraced the person I was created to be, but it's not that simple. That said, let's continue to unravel the pieces of fabric that were woven together to help shape my identity, starting with my grandma's imprint:

- "You better not bring anything in this house less than a B on your report card."

- "Don't you come in this house crying about somebody hit you; if they hit you, you better hit them back, or I'm going to whoop you."

- "If I find one dirty dish in that rack, you're going to wash every dish in that cabinet."

- "Don't let the streetlights come on, and you're not back in this house."

Oh, how sweet it would be to hear today my grandma say any one of those commands (yes, "commands"—she was something like a drill sergeant) to me.

My grandmother was a Christian woman who took us to church every Sunday and any day of the week that the church doors were open. But my grandmother was a force to be reckoned with. She was strict. She was a cussing Christian (maybe that's where I get it from). She was human, which meant she was perfectly flawed. I don't know her level of education, but she believed in us kids getting a good education. But when school wasn't in session, she let us have fun doing things that kids our age liked to do.

When we weren't at school or church, we were free spirits; laughing, running, getting dirty, and playing with our neighborhood friends. Back then, kids didn't stay in the house much. We would get together with our friends and play hopscotch, Simon Says, and kickball, to name a few, but my favorite outdoor activity was climbing trees. For you, maybe it was hiking, but the closest I got to hiking was using my upper body strength to climb up the moderately sized tree a few feet from our house. And more often than not, I'd hear, "Girl, if you don't get down from that (bleep bleep) tree, I'm going to beat your butt!" (I'm sure that last word started with an "a" and ended with an "s," but I'm trying to stick to the inexplicit version). "Ain't nobody taking you to the emergency room!" Grandpa would yell. And with all due respect, it went in one ear and out the other.

I told you I was a tomboy. I thought I was strong and tough! I would bench-press at least my body weight with my uncle's weight set. Until recently, I've always argued that I'm not competitive. Yet as far back as I can remember, I found great joy in racing and beating the boys in my neighborhood at any sport. I would even play tackle-football. As an adult, I still need and thrive off physical stimulation and healthy competition. Educationally, I remember how I loved getting homework. I wasn't big on classwork, largely because I liked to read, absorb it, and then process it, which is still true for me today. I wanted to make good grades. Not just because I was threatened, but I enjoyed learning. This was the fabric used to create Rochelle's foundation. Unfortunately, the smile currently spread across my face is quickly starting to dissipate as I mentally prepare to share the rest of Rochelle's journey.

I had my son on May 23, 1988, and started my summer job at Ahrens Vocational Center in June 1988. This was far from manual labor or anything that required critical thinking skills. Basically, we got paid for learning various vocations. My favorite was medical assistance. In this workshop, I remember writing down medical terminology on index cards to study for our weekly assessments. Some of those words I still can't pronounce, but what's important is that I knew what they meant. Nothing was retained that would qualify me as a doctor or registered nurse, but I do remember small facts like the human skeleton has 206 bones and the fibula is the long bone between the ankle and the knee. Honestly, I had no aspirations to go into the medical profession or go on *Jeopardy*, where any of this information would matter. Nonetheless, medical terminology fascinated me so much, it gave me the confidence to believe that I could at least be a medical assistant.

Another thing I recall about that program is that it was the first time I saw the classic movie *A Color Purple* starring Oprah Winfrey and Danny Glover. But one of the coolest things about being in this program was that it was my first job with benefits. As I tend to exaggerate, I should further explain that the benefits I'm referring to weren't medical insurance or a 401k plan; I was very grateful for the two free Tarc tickets that we received daily to ride the public bus to and from work and the free lunch that they provided. For a fourteen-year-old, this was a sweet package.

From there, I would attend Atherton High School in the upcoming school year. At the time, my baby and I were living in an apartment with my uncle, who was raising my sister and me; his girlfriend; and her three children. There were eight of us in a three-bedroom townhouse apartment, which worked for me. It was nice to be part of a larger family. Growing up, it was always just my grandma, grandpa, sister, and me in our household. So I'll always be grateful for my uncle's girlfriend for welcoming us into her home.

However, just like seasons change, chapters in life come to an end and new ones begin. Being a strong-willed and rebellious teenager—with a child—it was hard for any adult to try to finish raising me. How do you raise a child with a child? Not to mention, after everything I had witnessed with my grandmother, it made it very difficult to listen to anyone trying to teach me right from wrong. So, I thought, the worst thing that could happen to me had already happened; therefore, except for my son, life didn't have much meaning.

To that end, I'd wreak havoc wherever I stayed. Eventually, I got my own apartment at the age of sixteen. Yes, I lied about my age on the application, but the creepy landlord didn't care as long as I paid my $25 application fee along with the $100 deposit and $355 for the first month's rent. If you're as inquisitive as I am, you're wondering where I got the money from. Glad you asked. By this time, I was working every shift at McDonald's that my school schedule would allow me to work, and because I paid little to nothing for living expenses while staying with aunts and uncles, I was able to save up enough money to get a place for my son and me.

Shortly after, I met this guy through a mutual friend.

He and I started out as friends, talking on the phone for hours at a time, and after a few months, we started dating. Then, after about a year, he would stay over occasionally and helped pay my bills. His monetary contributions made it easier for me to work and stay in high school.

Then, winter would come: This guy was respectful, treated me nicely, was good to my son, and had a strong work ethic. However, unbeknownst to me, he had a personality-altering character flaw caused by drug abuse. Apparently, everyone in the neighborhood knew this but me. Other than sitting on the porch, going to work, going to school, and going to Dana's (our youngest daughter's godmother and one of my BFFs) apartment to get my hair done, I really didn't hang out in the neighborhood. I found out that he was on drugs when I went home one day to get the money for my rent and utility bill. I was devastated! It was all the money I had saved up. How was I going to pay my bills? Given that there was no sign of a break-in, I knew it had to be him.

When I discovered that the money was missing, he was still at work. Therefore, I had to wait all day (what felt like a lifetime) to confront him. When I did, he became very angry, defensive, and started choking me. After getting away from him, I called a friend for help. We got my key back, and needless to say, after that day, he and I would never speak again.

The demise of that relationship sounds simple, and for the most part, it was. However, the next relationship was not as easy to break away from. The father of my firstborn and I were never in a relationship, and I don't recall us ever communicating much, yet he would always seem to find me. I wasn't in love with him and I'm confident he wasn't in love with me, but he was part of my life.

Basically, it was Stockholm syndrome, which is "a psychological response wherein a captive begins to identify closely with his or her captors, as well as their agenda and demands."[7] Sounds irrational to you? How do you think I feel trying to explain this to you? Stockholm syndrome is another one of those terms that I wish was in my vocabulary when I was younger, because not knowing how to explain the dynamics of this connection, I only admitted to a handful of people that the sex was not consensual. In my ignorance, shame, and defeat, I allowed people to create and believe their own narrative that I was just another "fast" or promiscuous girl who got pregnant. This was far from the truth, but I didn't have the confidence or the energy to fight for myself. I had bigger battles to fight, getting rid of my son's father being one of them.

Now that I was seventeen and had some life experience under my belt, I also gained some confidence and self-worth. To that end, I was finally able to stand up for myself, reject his advances, and close that chapter in my life. A couple months later, I started getting sick all the time, and I quickly found out that it was morning sickness: I was pregnant again!

Single. No man. Two beautiful children depending on me. Although my sister and I were roommates at the time, I still struggled with my half of the bills, only working part-time at McDonald's. In full survival mode, I decided to drop out of school in the eleventh grade to work full-time at McDonald's. Reflecting back, I had no other options. Now that I was working full time, I was able to get daycare assistance to help pay for Jon and Jessie to go to daycare while I worked.

You may be thinking that this was a setback, but this was a strategic chess move, positioning myself for a checkmate. I had a dream! We had a purpose. This was a temporary state. I was always thinking ahead. I never set a goal that I couldn't accomplish. My plan was to work at McDonald's full time while babysitting for my neighbor who worked third shift and paid me $15 a day. My action plan was that when I reached eighteen years old, I'd have enough money saved up to move into Norfolk Apartments, where the rent would be cheaper because it would be based on my income. This break afforded me the opportunity to work part time, go to school full time, get my high school diploma, and after graduation, go to Jefferson Community College.

Interestingly enough, Norfolk Apartments were the same apartments where I had stayed with my uncle and his girlfriend. Although they were low-income housing, they were nice two- and three-bedroom townhomes with 1.5 baths and washer and dryer hookups. I loved it!

Prior to Norfolk, I had always lived over someone. In the apartment that my sister and I shared, we both grew irritated and frustrated by the woman who lived under us. She would hit the ceiling with a broom *every day*, encouraging us to make two toddlers (my son and nephew) simmer down. When I received my acceptance letter from Norfolk for my three-bedroom townhome, my big sister was happy for me, and from there, we both moved into our own apartments.

Now that I was eighteen-ish, I was going to school full time, and after being summoned to clean the baseboards (not a part of my job description) by my chauvinistic male boss (at that point in his life), I quit McDonald's without a two-week notice. I remember going out the side door, walking straight to the bus stop, hopping on the Tarc bus (public transportation), and going straight to the unemployment office to search for a new job.

After a few days, I started to get discouraged, maybe even depressed, when I was not working. Financially, we were okay because I always tried to keep emergency savings. At that time, I had enough money saved up for rent, utilities, and other necessities. But after some months, my savings quickly dwindled. Not to mention, I enjoyed working. Thankfully, this drought was short-lived. My sister was the manager at the Burger King in a hospital around the corner from where I was going to school, which made it convenient for me to leave work and go straight to class.

As it started to get closer to my graduation, life was starting to feel more balanced and things were looking up for the kiddos and me. Then, one day, on my way to work, someone hit me while I was driving my sister's car. It was totaled. After making sure I was okay, my sister was highly upset (to say the least) now that her only means of transportation was gone. The saving grace was that the man who hit me was overly apologetic and took full responsibility. As a result, not only was my sister able to get another car from the insurance, but I, too, was able to get a car with the insurance payout.

Shortly after this experience, I graduated from high school. The graduation was held at an arena in Louisville called Freedom Hall. It brings me great joy as I reflect on that day. I remember looking out into the audience at my family. I'll never forget how my sister and children were cheering for me as I walked across the stage to receive my high school diploma. What was equally special about that day was that I got to graduate with my cousin Dion, which meant the room was full of family support. Oh, what a happy day!

After high school graduation, I attended Jefferson Community College that upcoming semester, majoring in pre-law. Unfortunately, I had to drop out after attending a few semesters. By this time, I was working at a call center full time, going to college full time, and Jon and Jessie required more attention and help with schoolwork. To my dismay, it was time to hang up the Superwoman cape and better prioritize, which meant college was put on hold. But I never set a goal that I couldn't or wouldn't accomplish. Delay does not mean never!

Over the next twenty years, various fabrics were woven together to shape my identity. I won't bore you with all the details. What I will share is that I lost and found love. I accepted Christ and discovered who I am, or at least who I'm not. I worked at a couple of call centers, was a receptionist once, and would eventually work for the company that I recently resigned from after twenty-four years.

However, there are a few honorable mentions, especially for my hopeful single readers. After a couple of failed relationships, I practiced celibacy and enjoyed being single. I was a young woman who came into my own. I knew my worth and was willing to save myself for someone who could appreciate my mind, body, and soul. This happened around the age of twenty-six.

Let me go back a few years prior first. Working at my former company, my supervisor at the time and very close friend, Tajna, told me about this young man who went to her church and she thought we would be a great fit for each other. She went on and on about how he was on fire for God, very mature, and good-natured. All that said, she asked if it would be okay to get his number for me or give him my number. I said, "Sure, why not?" She was someone I respected and trusted. Unfortunately for him, she forgot to ask him when she went to Wednesday night Bible study that evening if he was okay with meeting me. To that end, when she circled back around to the conversation the next day, it dawned on me to ask his age. To my disappointment, he was exactly five years and five months younger than me. Having these stupid rules and a laundry list of do's and don'ts, I took back my agreement to meet him and went on with my single, happy life.

A few years later, Tajna invited me to her church, New Horizon. I loved it so much, I joined after only attending a few times, and it would eventually become my church home as an adult. From there, things moved quickly. After a few months, Jon and Jessie got baptized and I became an usher/greeter, taught Sunday school to the youth, and got involved with the women's ministry called Mothers and Daughters of Ruth. This place became a second home, and the members became my extended family. So it was only a matter of time before the guy (Jamel), that man-friend who Tajna wanted to hook me up with, would cross my path.

I can't remember if it was June or July, but it was in the summer that he and I started teaching vacation bible school (VBS) together. And since we lived in the same part of town, it just made sense (to me) that we ride together. Being the planner that I am, I'm known for confirming times, dates, etc. Therefore, being true to myself, while talking to him on the phone, I said, "You better pick me up tomorrow at 6:30." Let's just say I'm still waiting for him to pick me up.

Once the clock struck 6:15 p.m. and he wasn't at my apartment yet, out of concern, I called to see where he was at. To my surprise, he said, "I better not do anything!" I thought, "Oh, I can't believe he really didn't pick me up? He said that nobody was going to tell him what he better do." I guess it goes without saying that I was late to VBS that day, but that would be the start of a meaningful friendship. He started mentoring my son, picking him up for sports games and church events, and he and I would talk on the phone all the time for hours.

Then there was "the call." This phone conversation would change the rest of our lives. Over the weekend, he and his cousin came over to my apartment to fix my son's bike, and I told him that when he returned from a church conference he was going to in New Orleans, I would cook dinner for them. I wanted to express my gratitude, not just for fixing the bike but for taking my son under his mentorship. Interestingly enough, before leaving, we talked on the phone for several hours about everything from church to his romantic relationships and my lack thereof.

All of this was taking place outwardly, as two-way communication typically does, but inwardly, there was a soft audible voice I kept hearing saying, "He's going to be your husband." These unyielding words became annoying, but the voice itself wasn't foreign. This was the same voice that I had heard when I was a little girl, especially right before I fell asleep on a pile of blankets on the floor, that would say "Greater." At the time, I didn't know exactly what "Greater" meant. As I grew older and would still hear "Greater" periodically, sometimes at my lowest moments or at times when I contemplated settling, the interpretation became clearer. I trusted the voice. I never rudely dismissed it because it couldn't be explained logically or rationally.

As I reflect, the voice saved me from giving up or settling for mediocrity. Okay, back to "the conversation." Jamel and I were talking about how he wasn't in a committed relationship and felt like God was calling him to leave his romantic interests alone so that he could make space for God to truly bless him. Given that I was already on a similar path of being single to develop a more intimate relationship with God and to love myself, of course I encouraged him to do the same. But remember the soft voice? "He's going to be your husband"? It just wouldn't go away. But I'd be damned if those words were coming out of my mouth, at least not that evening.

Considering that we talked often, we were talking the next day about something random, and it started again: "He's going to be your husband." I had this overwhelming feeling that it wasn't going to go away until I spoke it. Keep in mind that although my friend and supervisor at the time had wanted to hook us up, once we met, neither of us expressed an interest in anything other than being friends.

For a moment, I want you to visualize having to tell someone that you're not even dating that you can't shake an inner voice that they're going to be your spouse. Okay, so I couldn't say, "I think you're going to be my husband." I couldn't even say, "I feel like you're going to be my husband," because that would have been a lie. I literally heard, "He's going to be your husband." "Alright, alright, I'll say it," I thought. And I did! Once I'd told him, there was complete silence.

Surprisingly, I wasn't embarrassed. Neither was it awkward or uncomfortable. We may have ended the call with "Good night." I hung up and I got ready for bed. But as soon as my head hit the pillow, I heard, "He just doesn't know yet." I thought, *Are you serious?*" Relieved that I'd done what I believe God was telling me to do, I was proud that I did it, and I was ready to put it behind me. Reader, do you ever feel like everything you do requires you to be bold and courageous? I do, too. I told you, I am not naturally courageous, but I am always led to do or say bold things.

Okay, back to the story. In part, I was glad that he didn't respond, because I wasn't ready to be in a relationship again. I was happily single. Stress-free! I hadn't felt that emotionally healthy in a long time. God was finally the loudest voice in my head. I was free from the heartache and drama that a lot of romantic relationships can bring. All that said, I was becoming annoyed as I heard this same voice say, "He just doesn't know yet." As the day progressed, I tapped into the left side of my brain, hoping to logically and rationally make sense of this, but to no avail. I was left with nothing but a strong sense that when he returned from his conference, he was going to confess that he felt the same way or he would never talk to me again because he thought I was cray-cray.

The verdict came in! He returned from his trip and he actually called the crazy lady—me. As promised, I cooked dinner for him and his cousin. And when we talked on the phone later that evening, he told me that the reason he couldn't utter a word when I'd said, "I hear this voice saying you're going to be my husband" was because after praying for God's guidance and letting go of those distracting relationships, he was astonished that God would bless him that fast. He admitted that once he'd hung up, he'd felt it too, but was in shock and disbelief.

Reader, this is where I would like to get a little more intimate and personal with you. Your religion, beliefs, or the lack thereof don't matter to me. For me and my house, we will always serve the Lord our God through His son Jesus Christ. Just know that my beliefs don't affect our relationship. I was intentional about writing this book for all people, not just Christians. Contrary to what is typically shown in the media about Christian values, most Christians believe in grace, compassion, repentance, and forgiveness for all people. Our core value is love. That said, if you have faith or believe strongly in something, stand strong in your convictions. Never let anyone discourage you from what you know to be true.

As long as there is human existence on planet Earth, the interpretation of the Bible will be argued. But what you can't argue with is the Spirit that lives inside of each of us. Some refer to it as gut instinct; others call it intuition. For Christians, we call it the Holy Spirit, and it becomes louder than anything else in our lives as we deepen our relationship with God. Throughout this book, I've told you that I've taken and administered a myriad of personality assessments, and every time I take one on spirituality, I score high in faith. In part, that means that I don't live by or only believe in what I can see; the Holy Spirit is real and He speaks to me.

One of the reasons I believe that I was able to hear "He's going to be your husband" so loudly, yet gentle and clear, was because I had eliminated all the other distractions, like unhealthy relationships, that were loud in my life. Another thing that I need to clarify is that I did not ask my now-husband of nineteen years to marry me—he asked me to marry him, sometime after I confessed what I believed to be true.

Once he'd responded to my bold statement after he returned from his trip, we never talked about it again. Neither did we immediately start dating. We continued as friends, getting to know each other better. Eventually, we started officially dating, and six months later, he proposed on Valentine's Day. To help seal the deal, he used a line from one of his favorite rappers and one of my celebrity crushes, Common: "It doesn't take all day to recognize sunshine." How could I argue with that?

There you have it, the Real Rochelle. Every situation, experience, persona, and piece of DNA that contributed to the person whom people know as Rochelle today was necessary for me to embrace my authenticity.

Moment of Reflection

Who is the authentic you? I mean, the real *you*? Not you the coach, you the mentor, you the teacher, you the parent, you the responsible sibling, you the pastor, you the entrepreneur, you the tattoo artist, you the activist, you the supervisor, you the manager, you the director, you the president, you the VP, you the CEO. No, no, no! Those are titles. *Who's behind the title?*

It's easy for your identity to get wrapped up into what you do to the point it starts to define who you are. Even worse, if the title is more respected, glamourous, or prestigious than you think you are, you'd rather take on that persona and hide the authentic you. Stop! If you're going to lead out of authenticity, it's time to get real with yourself. Now that you've made it to this pillar, there's no turning back. You have a strong foundation to stand on, even stronger to lead out of.

You know what's next, don't you? Yep, it's time to remove the mask and reveal who you really are. By now, you're familiar with completing sentence stems or incomplete sentences, right? This time, you're going to write a version of the story below customized to fit you—the authentic you. I've given you the framework. You just have to acknowledge what's true, dispel any lies, and write the story that best describes you. Here's an example:

I'm a leader. But I don't always feel like I have what it takes to lead in my home, to lead my team to the championship, to lead in the boardroom, to lead in the classroom, to lead those who look up to me, or to lead those I serve. Some mornings, I wake up and wonder if I'm good enough. I say to myself, "Why me?" I want to be authentic, I want to show people the real me, but what if they won't like me? What if they see how flawed I am? I'm scared. I need my job. I need this position. I need money to take care of my responsibilities.

Well, if I'm being honest, that's only partly true; I do what I do because it makes me feel good about myself. I feel in control. There're so many things in my life I can't control: my family dynamic, my past, my relationships, my mistakes, my weight, my diagnosis, my shape, my race, my sexual orientation, or my IQ, but when I'm operating in my element, I'm in control. I feel validated—until I make the wrong decision, we lose the game, or our test scores or metrics fall below our goal. Now I start to unravel. I start to feel inadequate, and the real me starts to show up under stress. Everything I've tried to hide and suppress starts to rise to the surface. I can no longer control my persona.

I go home and try to find my happy place with a favorite movie or show, exercise, a cold beer, a glass of wine, comfort food, or maybe a quick trip to the mall. Then the temporary satisfaction of these things starts to wear off, and I either go to sleep to avoid the pain or stay awake worrying about how to fix it. I awaken the next day and decide that I can no longer live up to the pressure of my title or public persona.

With every ounce of courage, I get out of bed, look in the mirror, and fall in love with my authentic self. Today, when I look into the mirror, I don't look the same. I have the "eye of the tiger." Today, I don't wake up with being a leader on my mind. I'm not thinking about solutions, emails, or deadlines. I feel a little bloated, but I don't try to suck my stomach in. I look in the mirror and I see every blemish and the puffiness under my eyes, yet I feel amazing! There's no pressure to cover up my flaws inwardly or outwardly. I feel as strong as a lion and as free as an eagle. There's no competition for me. I have no need to prove how smart I am, how good looking I am, or how charming I am. There's nothing to prove—I just am. I'm validated by the mere fact that I do the best I can with my appearance, gifts, talents, and personality.

I'm courageously removing the mask I've worn for way too many years, hiding the real me. When I show up, everyone is staring at me, but I'm not insecurely trying to figure out what they're looking at; from a place of confidence balanced with humility, I know what they see. In a sea full of personas, I stand out because I show up in my authenticity. Simply complex, I am! Onlookers marvel with curiosity in their eyes. Those I lead lean in closer as they sense truth and genuineness exuding from me.

Someone finally approaches me and says, "There's something different about you. Did you change your hair?" No. "Did you lose some weight?" No. They give me this long glare and say, "I don't know what it is, but you have this glow about you. I don't know what you did, but whatever it is, it's becoming on you." Finally, you smile, exhale, and reintroduce yourself. They give you this blank look, as to say "I already know who you are." Without stating the obvious, you turn and walk away and say to yourself, "So this is what it feels like to lead out of authenticity."

Reflections

Pillar XII: Simply Complex

Thank you for making me so wonderfully complex! Your workmanship is marvelous—how well I know it.
—Psalm 139:14 NLT

The Simply Complex pillar is not only essential for you to lead out of authenticity, but it's also your wild card. Wondering exactly what I mean? To be human is to be flawed, complicated, and messy. And no matter how simple you think you are, others will probably beg to differ. The opposite of simply complex is perfection.

But, if you've noticed, there's no pillar for perfect. Why? It would set you up for failure. Imperfect people embrace imperfect people. So to lead out of authenticity, you have to accept that you, too, are simply complex, which means you make mistakes, you're not always right, and sometimes you get jealous and judge others. There will be times when you can't get it right, won't get it right, or simply refuse to do it right. Is that not part of what makes you simply complex? Once you accept that, you'll unapologetically take the mask off and encourage those you lead to bury their personas and show up as their beautiful, imperfect, highly capable, and authentic selves.

I've just walked you through the day and the life of what it means for me to lead out of authenticity. As I wrap up this last chapter, sitting on the same chaise I started writing this book, I gaze at the sparsely decorated jade walls in my living room and I think how simple I am. Yet, depending on what I'm reading, writing, or imagining, sitting on the same chaise, staring at the same walls in my living room, I can feel complex. Could it be my interpretation of simple?

When I say I'm "simple," I'm thinking about how I've kept the same texturized hairstyle; it was once short and tapered, and now it's growing out in its natural texture, but when I don't wear it straight, it's still curly/coily. Personally, I think I have a modest, stylish look: It ranges from business to business-casual in the office. Otherwise, I love wearing a flattering top that's nestled into fitted jeans and a two-inch pump or wedge. When it comes to makeup, less is more. Nothing about me is overly flamboyant—not my appearance, house, car, or personality. But on occasion, I channel my inner Cyndi Lauper's "Girls Just Want to Have Fun," and instead of getting my accustomed French manicure or natural nail color, I put a mischievous smile on the face of my nail tech, Hoaly, when I say, "I'm getting a bright pink, white or red." Then, if I'm feeling really sassy, I change my hair color to a lighter blonde and lace my lips with bright pink lipstick. Interestingly enough to onlookers, I probably still look simple, but it's my way of expressing my versatility and uniqueness.

I'm drawn in by bright things, including the sun, but by now, I'm sure you know that I don't like to draw attention to myself. Sure, I like attention; I like to feel special to the people I'm in personal relationships with, but this doesn't mean I want to be the center of attention, which is why

I've never had a birthday party outside of a small gathering with close friends and family. As I reflect on my wedding reception and graduation party, I tried to convince myself that a celebration was in order so that I could let loose and embrace it, but I was totally awkward. I'm really a simple girl who will never forget my humble beginnings, while I have an appreciation for the finer things in life.

Now that I've shared my interpretation of what makes me simple, let me shed light on what I think makes me complex. Then you can determine for yourself if I'm simple, complex, or simply complex.

What makes me complex? One thing is that I want everyone, especially my husband, to read my mind. Early in our marriage, I was always disappointed, because after two to three years of being together, he should've known everything I wanted, needed, or liked, right? Ugh, wrong! Until this day, I'm not sure why I never got him a crystal ball, because it would've saved us both years of frustration.

Remember when I said that I don't need to be the center of attention, but I like to feel special to people I'm in a personal relationship with? Now, let's be clear: You should know how your loved ones, especially your significant other, like to be shown love. For me, I don't really like surprises or grandiose gestures. If you're familiar with *The Five Love Languages*, my top two are quality time and words of affirmation, and it took my husband years to figure out the latter. Truthfully, I didn't even know that words of affirmation was one of my love languages, or at least I didn't know the technical term, so how could I tell him? But admittedly, I could be quite petty when he didn't express love in the way I wanted to be loved.

It's taken almost twenty years, but I'm proud to say that I've gotten better at not expecting him to read my mind and can articulate what I need out of our relationship and others. Now it's only every now and then, when loved ones don't treat me the way I think they should treat me, that I start telling myself stories. Like the story I told myself on my twenty-fifth birthday when nobody either initiated a celebration or was available to celebrate with me. I promised myself that I'd never wait for anyone else to make me feel special, especially not on my birthday. Up until a few years ago, I stayed true to that.

As a matter of fact, everyone got so used to me either planning my own trip, going to get spa services, or simply planning and inviting everyone to go out to eat with me that people just stopped asking what I wanted to do for my birthday, except for one or two. For some reason (only God knows), a few birthdays ago, I had the nerve and audacity to want others to go out of their way to make me feel special. I must've forgotten my own commitment. Complex, right? Now, when I say "others," I'm mainly referring to my husband. I'll never forget it, and he probably won't either.

As the story goes, we had a date for breakfast immediately after his meeting at church. When he showed up, a couple of church members were with him, which was a welcomed surprise. But I felt like my husband should've known that this breakfast was not in lieu of a birthday celebration or gift. In my mind, this was just breakfast and it happened to be on my birthday. To that end, when we left breakfast, I just knew that my hubby had something else planned for us to do.

But to my surprise, when I asked, "What are we doing the rest of the day?" he said, "I'm going home to take a nap." *You're going to do what?* These words never flowed out of my mouth, but he probably wished they had, because I'm sure the silent treatment and my nonverbal demeanor were worse.

In addition to that, weeks before my birthday, my sister, Neki, had asked if it was okay if she made other plans that year because she had an opportunity to make some money doing one of her passions. "Of course," I said (isn't that the polite, selfless, humble thing to say?), not knowing that I was on the verge of reliving my sad, pitiful twenty-fifth birthday all over again. To make matters worse, by midday, when it seemed like nobody was going to initiate anything for my birthday, my internal volcano was on the brink of erupting. Now that I'm in my rational state of mind and reflect, look at the story I was telling myself: *Nobody cares that it's my birthday, so I must not be special.*

Prior to this fictional story I was telling myself, I had called our older children Jon and Jessie earlier in the day to see if they wanted to go to dinner with me, and they graciously obliged. But now that the volcano was literally running over, I even canceled dinner. My poor children were so upset. They genuinely wanted to go out to celebrate my birthday. Then, later that evening around 9 p.m., my sister and friend Keisha came over with a cake and card, and I didn't even want to get out of bed.

Yes, as I reflect, I feel ashamed for acting like that, but as much as I wanted to leave this part of my story out, it helps paint the picture of how I can be complex. That said, I reluctantly got out of bed so that they could sing happy birthday, and I watched them eat cake and ice cream. Given that my current state was less than enjoyable to be around, my guests didn't stay long. After they left, it was late, but my son still came over and took me out for appetizers and a drink, hoping that I would feel special on my birthday. Thank you, Jon! Mission accomplished. If you haven't figured out by now why wanting people to read my mind makes me complex, you, too, may be guilty of occasionally falling into the same trap. Maybe I'm not the only one who is simply complex.

One thing that inspired me to write this book was my passion for bringing the best out of people, starting with being authentically who they are—in part because this is something that I've always struggled with. I thought about why some people pursue their dreams, while others don't dream at all. Why some people are successful, yet others always seem to struggle. Why some people appear to have it all but are still unhappy, while others have very little but have great joy is what led me to explore one's identity and what it means to lead out of authenticity.

From the time we were conceived, our identity was already being shaped by DNA and further developed by environment, including every interaction and encounter that we have in our lifetime. This means that our identity plays a major role in how we perceive ourselves. And how we perceive ourselves has a lot to do with how far we will go in life. Will we settle for being mediocre and just getting by? Or will we strive to be the best at whatever we do, whether it's cleaning homes, doing factory work, working in corporate America, or being a stay-at-home parent, full-time student, fast food worker, preacher, teacher, tattoo artist, police officer, social worker, coach, comedian, or entrepreneur? How will you allow your identity to influence what you do and how you show up? For me, I'm going to accept that I'm simply complex and use it to lead out of authenticity.

Moment of Reflection

You made it! What did it take for you to get here? Not to the last chapter of this book. What did it take for you to acknowledge and accept that you have a persona(s)? Once you'd acknowledged it, what emotions did you experience? Given that we live in a society where everyone proudly proclaims, "I'm just keeping it real," were you in denial? Do you play on words? Okay, let's say you don't have a persona; do you always show up as your authentic self? If so, good for you. I'm surprised you made it this far in the book, so give this copy to someone who struggles with authenticity. Just kidding, keep it and buy them a copy—you might need it one day.

Leading out of authenticity is no easy challenge. Not for those who want to project a spot-free image, an image that has been predetermined of what is acceptable or not by society. This new discovery of self doesn't happen overnight, and it has to be cultivated daily. How much easier would life be if one day we woke up and boldly confessed: "I'm taking off the mask and I'm living as the person I was created to be—leading out of authenticity." Oh no, my friend. I wish. Do you always feel confident? Do you always feel attractive? Do you always feel creative? Do you always feel smart? Surely not. If you do, you might suffer from a mental disorder called narcissism, and that wouldn't even be entirely true, given that narcissism comes from a place of insecurity.

It is completely natural to not always feel at your best, and being authentic is no different. I believe that our humility comes from our imperfections and shortcomings. Imagine if you were always at your best. It would be challenging for you to see any good in others. Why? To be human is to have flaws, make mistakes, and struggle with some type of insecurity. Therefore, if you didn't have weaknesses, you in all your glory and self-righteousness would constantly judge or pity others for not being perfect like you.

Frankly, I wish it didn't have to be that way. Wouldn't it be empowering and reassuring to always be confident and sure of yourself? Unfortunately, Superman isn't the only one crippled by kryptonite, but don't allow your weaknesses and fear of rejection to stop you from unleashing your superpower: authenticity. I don't know about you, but I would love to never struggle with insecurities or needing validation from others. I wish I could wake up every morning and embrace my authentic self.

But the truth is, I start each day with the same positive reinforcement that I'm giving you: You have the courage and confidence to lead out of authenticity, balanced with enough humility to encourage others to do the same.

Acknowledgments

On this journey called life, I have encountered many experiences, people, and places that have helped shape the person I am today. And as I continue to become the person I was created to be, I am grateful to all the amazing people who have loved me unconditionally despite my shortcomings and character flaws.

I would specifically like to acknowledge my beloved family, who have lived through all my personas and yet are still gracious to me. I feel most loved and honored by all of you for allowing me to share parts of your stories as well. To my oldest son, Jon: there would be no me without you. After Grandma died, life was no longer worth living, but the first time I felt you move in my stomach, I knew I had to fight for our lives. To my middle daughter, Jessie: you brought a glimmer of hope and light into our world that served as notice that life would keep getting better. To my youngest daughter, Dejah: you brought joy into our home and hearts during a season in life when we all were in desperate need of sunshine. To my sister, Sheniquia: you have always been my protector, confidante, and friend. To my great-niece, Zari: although your daddy, Fonnie, is no longer with us, you fill our lives with his spirit through your humor, smile, and bigger-than-life personality, just like he did. To my dear mother-in-law, Jackie: you have always treated me like your own daughter and Jon and

Jessie as your first grandchildren, and I hope you know that we love you to the moon and back.

I would be remiss to not give a special acknowledgment to my editor, Diedre. Diedre, it would have taken me much longer to finish my manuscript without you. You are a godsend. It was your kind, calm, and gentle spirit that helped me trust humans again and gave me the confidence I needed to finish my manuscript.

There are so many family members and good friends whose names I won't mention for fear of leaving out someone who is special to me, but I hope you know who you are.

Now, staying true to the adage, "Save the best for last." To the person who saw my gifts and potential when I didn't see them in myself; the person who saw "my crazy" and married me anyway; the person who challenges me to be uncomfortable and to be a better version of myself; and the person who holds me when I cry but helps put my armor on when I have to face the battles of life. To my husband, Jamel: you are my biggest champion and best friend. I thank you and everyone aforementioned for holding me accountable to pursue my dreams and be true to my authentic self.

In loving memory of my grandmothers, Margaret Jones and Leila Bowman-Jimerson; my parents, Alvin Jones and Debra Bowman; and my nephew, Stephon Bowman.

Endnotes

1   Brené Brown, *Dare to Lead: Brave Work. Tough Conversations. Whole Hearts* (New York: Random House, 2018), 10.

2   Children and Families of the Incarcerated Fact Sheet," Rutgers University National Resource Center on Children & Families of the Incarcerated, accessed November 24, 2020, https://nrccfi.camden.rutgers.edu/files/nrccfi-fact-sheet-2014.pdf.

3   "Children and Families of the Incarcerated Fact Sheet."

4   "Smoketown History & Heritage," Smoketown Voice, accessed November 24, 2020, www.smoketownvoice.com/smoketown-history.

5   I intentionally use the word "probably" because I'm not a therapist. Therefore, I'm not trying to psychoanalyze you. Similar to the other exercises I've encouraged you to do in this book, I'm asking questions to challenge you to think deeply and reflect on your perception of self.

6   Travis Bradberry and Jean Greaves, E*motional Intelligence 2.0* (San Diego, CA: TalentSmart, 2009), 2.

7   "Stockholm Syndrome," Britannica, accessed November 24, 2020, www.britannica.com/science/Stockholm-syndrome.